DISCOVERING
WYCHWOOD

WOODBANK AND UNDERSTOREY IN WYCHWOOD

edited by
Charles Keighley

DISCOVERING
WYCHWOOD

WYCHWOOD
PRESS

To past and present
———— *stewards of Wychwood* ————

Our books may be ordered from bookshops or (post free) from
Jon Carpenter Publishing, Alder House, Market Street, Charlbury, OX7 3PH
01608 811969

Credit card orders should be phoned or faxed to 01689 870437 or 01608 811969

Please send for our free catalogue

First published in 2000 by
The Wychwood Press, an imprint of Jon Carpenter Publishing,
Alder House, Market Street, Charlbury, Oxfordshire, OX7 3PH

ISBN 1 902279 09 3

Designed by Bibliofile, Chipping Norton, 01993 830122
Printed in England by J. W. Arrowsmith Ltd, Bristol

Contents

LIST OF CONTRIBUTORS

RICHARD BIDGOOD, formerly a bank official, on retirement studied for the Certificate in English Local History at the University of Oxford Department for Continuing Education and is now a researcher with the Oxfordshire Museum Service.

CHRISTINE BLOXHAM, B.A., A.M.A., formerly Curator of Banbury Museum and Assistant Keeper of Antiquities at the Oxfordshire Museum from 1974 to 1983, is an author, broadcaster and lecturer specialising in Oxfordshire subjects. She is the author of *The World of Flora Thompson*.

NICK DALBY, Dip.La., is Landscape and Forestry Officer with West Oxfordshire District Council.

BELINDA FLITTER, B.Sc., M.A.(L.Arch.), is the Wychwood Project Officer.

AMANDA HOPWOOD, B.A., B.Phil., L.D., M.L.I., is a landscape architect with BHWB Environmental Design and Planning.

CHARLES KEIGHLEY, M.A., is a local solicitor with an interest in architectural and landscape history. He is the Secretary of the Wychwood Project.

VICKY PRICE, B.Sc., works for the Farming and Rural Conservation Agency and is also studying for a Diploma in Environmental Conservation at the University of Oxford Department for Continuing Education.

BERYL SCHUMER, B.Sc., M. Phil., formerly a biochemist, became 'hooked' on local history after attending the University of London Extra-mural Department. She subsequently studied, in her spare time, at Leicester University. She is the principal historian of Wychwood and her researches have stimulated interest in the area.

ALAN SPICER, M.Sc., is a retired university lecturer with an interest in the history and conservation of the countryside. He is co-author of the Oxfordshire Country Walks series of books and Chairman of the Wychwood Project.

KATE TILLER, B.A., Ph.D., is Reader in English Local History at the University of Oxford Department for Continuing Education. Her teaching has stimulated many local historians.

MARY WEBB, M.A., studied at Oxford Polytechnic and at Reading University where she took an M.A. in Landscape History. She is co-author of the Oxfordshire Country Walks series of books, and is currently Environmental Co-ordinator at Oxford Brookes University.

Foreword

The Wychwood Project is one of the most ambitious of many recent initiatives to safeguard, improve and assist the public understanding of the Oxfordshire environment. It was a wonderful idea of about five years ago which is now being developed in an imaginative, efficient and realistic way. Dreamed up by local volunteers, it has won a great deal of support in West Oxfordshire, and been endorsed by public bodies in the county and at national level. In the year 2000 it is creating a 37 mile circular footpath around much of the Wychwood area, with the help of the Millennium Festival Fund. New woodlands are being established and other habitats restored. The Project is being seen as a model for other areas and is even attracting international interest.

A notable feature of the Project, indeed one of its great strengths, is that it embraces every aspect of the Forest: its social and economic history; its ecology and land-use; its interpretation; and its possibilities for the future.

This book, another welcome manifestation of the effectiveness of those involved in the Project, is also wide-ranging. It will expertly introduce some to the Forest; it will deepen the knowledge of others. It is a guide and it is a reference book.

For me it is a great pleasure to be associated with such an excellent book and such a splendid undertaking. And I consider it very appropriate, as the Queen's representative in Oxfordshire, that I should serve as a Patron of a project which celebrates an area defined by its former status as a Royal Forest.

HUGO BRUNNER

The beech avenue, Cornbury, from Vernon
J. Watney's book *Cornbury and the Forest
of Wychwood*, 1910

Introduction

In the thirteenth century the boundaries of Wychwood Forest were the River Glyme to the east, the River Windrush to the south and west, and the smaller Sars Brook to the north.

A Forest, in the medieval sense, was a region where the king had the right to keep deer and make Forest laws. Wychwood was such a royal Forest. This legal concept of a Forest should not be confused with woodland. Nevertheless, Wychwood happened to be one of the most wooded royal Forests in England, and remnants of its woodlands still exist throughout the area, for example around High Lodge in Blenheim Park to the east, Cogges Wood near Witney to the south, Widley Copse near Fulbrook to the west and at Ditchley to the north. The area of woodland lying between Charlbury, Leafield and Finstock – nowadays known to many as 'Wychwood Forest' and marked as such on the Ordnance Survey maps – is another such remnant which remained under the crown until the nineteenth century. As well as woodland, however, the medieval Forest included meadows, cultivated open fields, heaths and downs – a wide range of habitats.

The aim of this book is to help you discover Wychwood.

In Chapter 1 Beryl Schumer gives a brief history of Wychwood before the enclosures. Disafforestation – technically the reduction from the legal status of Forest to that of ordinary land – has taken place over many centuries in Wychwood, but much of the Forest woodland was disafforested and cleared as recently as 1857. In Chapter 2 Kate Tiller discusses the ramifications of the nineteenth-century transformation of the Forest. Chapter 3 gives a brief description of local Forest industries and Chapter 4 gives a sample of Wychwood's legends, stories and folklore.

Our world is different from that of the self-confident nineteenth-century 'improvers' described by Kate Tiller. We are concerned with global warming, agricultural uncertainty, international markets and increasingly short-term demands. Sometimes it appears as if the individual is powerless to change things for the better, even on his or her own doorstep. Although Wychwood is a pleasing and relatively rich part of rural England, even here species are declining and the quality of much of the landscape is beginning to deteriorate. Locally, wildlife under threat includes the corn bunting, grey partridge, lapwing, turtle dove, linnet, flycatcher, reed bunting, hare, water vole and native crayfish. As a first step to halt this decline, we must take stock of what we have. In Chapter 5 Alan Spicer describes the natural history of today's Wychwood, by describing the various habitats of the area. Fortunately, much historic landscape can still be discovered, as Mary Webb shows in Chapter 6.

The Wychwood Project, described in Chapter 7, is working with the support of local people to restore the rich patchwork of landscapes and habitats that are so distinctive of Wychwood. Drawing on the area's history, ecology and cultural identity it aims to create a sustainable environment for the future. Chapter 8 gives some practical suggestions for strengthening the character and wildlife of the Wychwood landscape.

Whether you are a visitor or a resident, there is much to explore. Chapter 9 describes several walks to help you get to know Wychwood better and is followed by a Gazetteer of towns, villages and hamlets in the Wychwood area.

My thanks are due to all those who have written chapters and articles and especially Beryl Schumer whose knowledge and help has made this book possible. Several contributors to the book spoke at day schools about Wychwood held at the University of Oxford Department for Continuing Education in November 1998 and April 1999. Other speakers included James Bond, John Broad, Oliver Rackham and Stephen Warnock. They have all made an indirect contribution.

The illustrations and photographs come from a variety of sources, including the authors of the chapters as well as Ken Betteridge, Craig Blackwell, Marc Dando, Amanda Henriques, Louise Spicer and David West.

In addition I would like to thank Jane Corbett, The Ditchley Foundation, Eric Dougliss, Michael Freeman, David Holme and North Leigh School, Martin Jarratt, Sue Jourdan, Robert Keeling, Graham Nelson, Nick and Sarah Potter, Sue Richards, Geoff Smith, Roy Stephens, Keith Wheal and FWAG in Berkshire and Oxfordshire for their help.

Finally, I would like to thank Oxfordshire County Council, West Oxfordshire District Council, Oxfordshire CPRE, the Greening Lamborn Trust and the Marc Fitch Fund, all of whose support has made publication possible.

CHARLES KEIGHLEY

A brief history of Wychwood before the Enclosures

BERYL SCHUMER

For many centuries Wychwood has been the most important feature of the landscape of West Oxfordshire, or at least of that part of the region which lies between the river Windrush and the smaller river Glyme; and although much of it was cleared in the middle of the last century, it still has a romantic appeal, conjuring up visions of a dark, mysterious and possibly dangerous piece of woodland.

Of course the name has nothing to do with witches, nor even wych elms or wych hazel; it derives from that of an Anglo-Saxon kingdom, based in the Severn valley, the land of the Hwicce. However this in itself is a mystery, because all the other records of that kingdom, and there are many, imply that its territory stopped at the boundary of Gloucestershire, and the name is the only evidence for any connection between the Hwicce and West Oxfordshire. That is one puzzle posed by Wychwood; another is why by Domesday there should have been any woodland remaining at all.

WYCHWOOD BEFORE DOMESDAY

It used to be thought that any woodland existing at the time of the Norman Conquest was just the remnant of vast forests (the 'wildwood') which had presumably colonised the whole of England after the retreat of the ice in the post-glacial period. Now the increasing amount of archaeological evidence has proved beyond doubt that the primeval wildwood, in Southern England at least, had almost certainly been largely cleared in the Bronze Age, whilst in the four centuries when the Romans were in Britain the amount of woodland in the landscape would not have been very different from that present today. Wychwood itself is a good example of this. Hidden among the woods which survive there are at least two long barrows dating from the Neolithic period, and several round barrows which were presumably constructed in the Bronze Age. Barrows were meant to be seen, and the area in which they were built must have been open land at the date of their construction. Indeed, the soil profile immediately below a long barrow excavated at Ascott-under-Wychwood suggested that cleared grassland had existed prior to the creation of the barrow.

11

The Iron Age was a period of considerable activity in the Wychwood area. In the period immediately preceding the arrival of the Romans the inhabitants of the locality were sufficiently numerous and powerful to construct a series of banks and ditches, now known as Grim's Ditch, which formed the largest territorial enclosure of any period in the British Isles. This would not, and could not, have been constructed in a totally wooded landscape, although the area may not have been completely cleared. Several large Roman villas were later built within this enclosure, including those at North Leigh, Stonesfield, Fawler, Shakenoak and Ditchley. Roman villas or settlement sites have been discovered in other places in what was later to be Wychwood Forest, although these are not as numerous as in the Grim's Ditch area and are mostly found in the river valleys, with only one Roman farmhouse (at Brize's Lodge) and scattered finds on the higher ground which was wooded in the Middle Ages.

All of this implies that any primeval woodland which may have existed in West Oxfordshire had almost certainly been cleared at least once. Wychwood is not unique in this, for the same has been found in most other parts of England. This clearance still creates problems for historians when they try to find an explanation for the fact that some areas 'tumbled down to woodland' in the centuries between the end of Roman rule and the arrival of the Normans, while others remained as open, cultivated land. Worsening climate, with a retreat to the best land, is one explanation offered and unsettled political conditions locally another, but the true story may never be known. Certainly in the Wychwood area the villa at Ditchley was inhabited until the fifth century, and that at Shakenoak until perhaps the eighth century. This period is a source of considerable academic discussion, but possibly the inhabitants ranched cattle in neglected farmland with a gradual encroachment of woodland into what could be described as a savannah landscape.

A study of local place names, especially those containing the elements *tun* and *leah*, suggests which areas may have been wooded in the late Saxon period. It is now accepted that those names contrast a settlement in an open, cleared environment, the *tun*, and one in a woodland setting, the *leah*. Broadly the *leah* settlements occur within the area between the Glyme and the Thames-Windrush, within a circle of *tun* names, for example Hailey, Leafield and Ditchley surrounded by Ducklington, Chadlington and Kiddington. The *leah* settlements were apparently of less importance than the *tuns*. In the Wychwood area many of the *tun* settlements had large amounts of woodland within their territory, but the *tun* always seems to have been surrounded by its

arable fields and separated from its woodland, whereas the *leah* was at the edge of, or within, woodland or heath.

ROUND BARROW AT LEAFIELD

THE ROYAL FOREST

At the time of the Norman Conquest, there was a large amount of woodland in that part of West Oxfordshire which lay between the Glyme and the Windrush, and it was to become a royal Forest. Forest is here used in its medieval sense, as a place where the deer were reserved for the king's use, and where the Forest law, laid down for the purpose of protecting both the deer and their environment, operated in addition to the common law of the land, with Forest officials and special Forest courts to administer it through separate districts or bailiwicks. There were also a few private Forests, usually known as 'chases', where the deer and forestal rights belonged to an individual, usually a bishop or great lord; however there were none of these in Oxfordshire, although the Bishop of Winchester's woods in Witney manor came to be called Witney Chase.

This concept of a Forest should not be confused with woodland. Royal Forests were not exclusively wooded, and indeed the bounds of the royal Forests of Exmoor and Dartmoor seem to have been drawn to exclude the surrounding woods. As we shall see, Wychwood Forest was far from entirely wooded, and yet it was one of the most wooded royal Forests in England. These Forests were rarely sited on prime agricultural land.

No records survive of the creation of a Forest. The first boundaries were usually physical, rivers or streams, to ensure that subjects knew when they were entering those regions where deer were protected.

However, the Forest boundary did not remain fixed; it could be, and on several occasions was, changed at the will of a king or when the king was forced to change it by pressure from his subjects. The new boundary was often described as a 'perambulation', when royal officials and local representatives would literally walk or ride the bounds. This was especially important when the new boundary did not follow natural features but took an intricate route along existing manorial or other boundaries.

At no time did the area within a Forest correspond to the extent of the woodland in the region.

The following are examples of the extent of the Forest as stated at different times:

Limits & bounds of the forest of Whichwood [1552]

First from the wall of Woodstoke Park and thence to the bridge called Bladenebrige [at Hanborough] and so by the water of Bladenbroke [river Evenlode] to the water mill of Eynsham and so to le Grymsham [at Witney] and so thence by the rivulet called Wynerusshewater [Windrush] to the bridge of the borough of Burforde... which extends in length 12 miles, and from the bridge of Burforde by known limits and bounds to the water of Glyme and so thence to the wall of Woodstoke Park, which extends in length 12 miles, in width in divers places 7 miles and in other places 1 mile...

Whichwood Forest [1638]

...extends to the towns of Old and New Woodstock, Bladon, Easham [Eynsham], Stanton Harcourt, Southleigh, Cogges, Witney, Widford Langley, Minster Lovell, Shipton under Whichwood, Pudlicote, Fyfield, Taynton, Idbury, Bruerne, Sarsden, Deane, Chadlington, Spellsbury, Charlbury, Fawler, Willcote, Northleigh, Hanborowe, Combe, Stonesfield, Dytchleye, Taston, Fulwell, Neat Enstone, Clyvely, Radford, Upper Kiddington, Asterley, Glympton, Wootton, Hordley and Durnford and their precincts...

Actually both of the extracts given above are misleading – the 1638 description comes from a time when Charles I was trying to put the clock back three hundred years, and it includes many places which had been declared to be out of the Forest (that is, no longer under Forest law) around 1300, and others (Hordley, Dornford and Old and New Woodstock) which had not been in the Forest since 1219. However, apart from those, the document gives a good idea of how large the Forest was during the thirteenth century. The 1552 bounds represent the area over which the royal Forester still claimed some sort of authority at that date, although it too includes land which had been disafforested around 1300.

Forests were instituted by William the Conqueror, following a continental tradition. Essentially the king was stamping his authority on his subjects by keeping deer for his own use on large tracts of land which was often in the use of other people. Soon Forests became the supreme status symbol.

Oxfordshire's Forests are recorded in Domesday Book. Wychwood was one of several; others included Shotover and later Bernwood. Although the Forests west of the Cherwell are named together as Woodstock, Cornbury and Wychwood, it is not known exactly what the names meant at that date. Woodstock later came to be used for Woodstock Park and Cornbury for Cornbury Park, leaving Wychwood as a general name for the Forest and the woodland. However in the earliest twelfth-century records the Forest is named not as Wychwood but as Cornbury and the annual *census*, the sum which the Forester paid to the crown, continued to be paid under that name until 1499. The name Wychwood, as referring to the whole Forest area, first appears in the records in 1184 and by around 1220 it had become the term used everywhere except in the *census* entry in the Pipe Rolls.

It is difficult to interpret the dimensions given for the Oxfordshire Forests in Domesday Book and to know exactly how large they were at that date. The kings who followed William I enlarged the Forests until, in the reign of King John, Wychwood extended from the Thames northwards to the stream which forms the northern boundary of Great Tew, and from the Cherwell west to the county boundary – that is from Kelmscott to Swerford, and from Kidlington to west of Burford. This, of course, did not mean that there were any more trees in the landscape, merely that there was a much greater area in which the deer were allowed to roam unmolested, and from whose inhabitants the king could get revenue in the form of fines for offences against the Forest law. This was a major source of royal income at that period, although later other forms of taxation became more important.

As a result of pressure from the barons at the time of Magna Carta, King John agreed to take these boundaries back to where they had been in 1155, and the bounds then became the Windrush, the county boundary, the Sars Brook, the Glyme, the lower Evenlode and the Thames.

The Forest had always included many settlements and woods belonging to owners other than the king, and by the end of the thirteenth century they were pressing to have their land and woods

manor	hidage	plough-lands	estimated acreage	wood	pasture	meadow
Ascott	$4\frac{1}{2}$	7	1440	-		16 ac
	6	5		3 f x 2 f	4 ac	15 ac
Asthall*	11	15	1260	13 f x 10 f		137 ac
Bladon	5	7	840	1 L x $\frac{1}{2}$ L		14 ac
Bloxham	$34\frac{1}{2}$			$13\frac{1}{2}$ f x 9 f		
Chadlington	$2\frac{1}{2}$	2	480	–		
	$2\frac{1}{2}$	2		–		3 ac
Charlbury	no information					
Churchill	20	20	2400	–	120 ac	170 ac
Cogges	5	8	960	18 f x 6 f	3 f x 1 f (21 ac)	11 f x 2 f
Combe	1	4	480	$1\frac{1}{2}$ L x $1\frac{1}{2}$ L		15 ac
Dean & Chalford	8	8	960	1 L x 2 f		13 ac
	3	3	360			4 ac
Enstone	24	26	3160	1 L x $\frac{1}{2}$ L	4 f x 2 f (56 ac)	50 ac
Eynsham	$15\frac{1}{2}$	18	2160	$1\frac{1}{2}$ L x 1 L 2 f	100 ac	255 ac
Fifield	5	7	840	–	1 L x 1 L (1010 ac)	24 ac
Fulbrook	12	15	1800	6 f x 2 f	10 f x 3 f (210 ac)	63 ac
Glympton	10	6	720	6 f x 6 f		18 ac
Hanborough	9	12	1240	7 f x 6 f		100 ac
Hensington	$1\frac{1}{4}$	1	480	6 ac		3 ac
	$2\frac{1}{2}$	2		5 ac		1 f x $\frac{1}{2}$ f
	$1\frac{1}{4}$	1		6 ac		3 ac
Idbury	14	12	1440	–	7 f x 7 f (345 ac)	60 ac
Kiddington	$1\frac{1}{2}$	2	960	5 f x 1 f		12 ac
	5	6		1 L x 3 f		2 ac
Kidlington	14			3 f x 3 f		
Milton-u-W	4	4	600	–	2 f x $\frac{1}{2}$ f (7 ac)	6 ac
	1	1		1 L x 4 f		2 ac
Minster (Lovell)	7	10	1560	1 L x 4 f		78 ac
North Leigh	10	10	1200	$1\frac{1}{2}$ L x 1 L		90 ac
Sarsden*	20	28	3360	1 L x 4 f	4 f x 4 f (110 ac)	155 ac
Shipton-u-W*	$33\frac{3}{4}$	53	6300	Kings enclosure	no information	
Spelsbury	10	16	1920	1 L x 7 f	36 ac	32 ac
Stanton*	26	23	2760	1 L x $\frac{1}{2}$ L	200 ac	200 ac
Stonesfield	1	1	120	5 f x 2 f		-
Swinbrook	$4\frac{1}{2}$	3	360	3 f x 1 f		3 ac
Taynton	10	15	1800	1 L x $\frac{1}{2}$ L	1 L x 4 f (335 ac.)	170 ac
Wilcote	1	2	120	4 f x 1 f		12 ac
Witney*	30	24	2880	3 L x 2 L		100 ac
Wootton	5	10	1920	Kings enclosure	no information	
	5	6		–	13 ac	13 ac

KEY **f** a furlong, 220 yards or 200 metres
L a league, about 1.5 miles or 2.4 kilometres
ac an acre, 0.4 hectares
ploughlands number of ploughs required to till that particular manor
hidage number of hides
* at that time larger than the modern counterpart parish

Extracted from John Morris' *Domesday Book: Oxfordshire*

freed from the control of the royal officials who policed the Forest. King Edward I was eventually forced to agree, being in need of the support of his barons for his wars, and Wychwood was split into three parts. One of these was based on the royal palace and park at Woodstock, and consisted of that and the royal manors and woods near it. Another consisted of the northern part of Witney manor (Hailey and Crawley), which belonged to the Bishop of Winchester, with the addition of part of North Leigh. The third consisted of the royal park of Cornbury with an adjacent area of royal demesne woodland, that is, wood which belonged directly to the crown and did not form a part of any manor, royal or otherwise. This section also included Langley, the home of the Forester of Wychwood, and part of Finstock. It is not known why this, and part of North Leigh, remained within the Forest when other land in private hands was taken out of it.

Although these bounds were eventually accepted, after much dissension between the Crown and the lords, the king kept some residual rights over the woods which had been disafforested, in that he still claimed the right of feed for the deer. The 1552 bounds quoted above actually give a rough idea of the extent of the land over which these residual rights were claimed.

In 1480 the woods around Woodstock Park 'from the town of

Charlbury to the said park and from the water of Combe to the water of Glyme', which had previously been within Wychwood Forest, were declared to be a 'New Forest' and given to a Keeper who was usually also the custodian of the Park. This New Forest is recorded as having been disafforested by Richard III and, in spite of the 1552 definition of the extent of the Forest quoted above, the people of the vicinity seem to have regarded themselves as no longer under Forest law. Consequently there was a protest in the seventeenth century when James I reimposed assart rents – that is, a charge on any land which had been cleared from woodland for agriculture – which had lapsed, and especially when Charles I re-instituted the Forest Courts. As a result of these protests new descriptions of the bounds were made in 1622 and repeated in 1649, and from these the only area to remain as Forest was the royal demesne woodland – although the woods which lay next to that, the 'purlieu' woods, were still subject to the right of feed for the deer. Previously the Forest had probably been without fences, so that the deer could stray into adjacent fields and pastures, but this area, both Forest and purlieus, was separated from the rest of the countryside by a wall which was begun in the reign of James I although not completed until 1690. Some traces of this can still be found.

The demesne woodland remained as the royal Forest until the middle of the nineteenth century. It is this which has entered into the consciousness both of the people of the locality and of others as 'the Forest of Wychwood'. The last stage of its history is told in Chapter 2.

ASSARTING, THE EARLY CLEARANCES FOR AGRICULTURE

The map on pages 20–21 shows the extent of the Forest, and the likely extent of the woodland, in the mid-twelfth century. Together, the woodlands and heaths approached 50% of the Forest area – a high proportion for an English Forest. 'Assarting', the creation of farmland by clearance and encroachment on the woodland of the Forest, began to reduce this proportion.

Fines for assarting had become a source of continuing revenue, as the figures for the assart rents for 1249/50 show. By this time much of the woodland in Witney manor had already been cleared, and assarting continued there for the rest of that century until only Chase Woods in Crawley and Singe Wood remained. Other assarts were made in Ramsden, Finstock, North Leigh, Fawler, Charlbury, Enstone and the King's own manors of Combe, Stonesfield and Wootton. Eventually the woodland of Wychwood was split into three separate parts. North of the Evenlode there was a scatter of woods and assarts stretching from

Woodstock towards Taston and Fulwell; south of the Evenlode the wood and heath belonging to Eynsham and Cogges was separated by assart fields from the largest surviving piece of woodland, the demesne Forest and the woods around it.

In the middle of the fourteenth century the Black Death stopped the assarting and even led to the shrinkage or desertion of several villages around the perimeter of the woodland, for example at Tangley and Tilgarsley.

ASSART RENTS, 1249/50

Ascott	
From Roger Douly for 2 acres of winter wheat	2s
From Adam le Fulur of Ditchley for $1\frac{1}{2}$ roods of oats	$2\frac{1}{4}$d
From Alice widow of Reginald of Fulwell for $\frac{1}{2}$ acre and 1 rood of oats	$4\frac{1}{2}$d
From John Fox for $\frac{1}{2}$ acre & $\frac{1}{2}$ rood of oats	$3\frac{3}{4}$d
Asterleigh	
From Ralph de Saucey for 1 acre & 1 rood of oats	$7\frac{1}{2}$d
From the same Ralph for $\frac{1}{2}$ acre of oats	4d
From Gilbert Jop for 1 rood of oats	$3\frac{1}{2}$d
From Roger Pass for 2 acres of oats	12d
From Henry War for 2 acres of oats	12d
Charlbury	
From John son of the reeve for $\frac{1}{2}$ rood of oats	$3\frac{3}{4}$d
Fawler	
From Nicholas de Anvers for 1 acre of oats	6d
From Richard Schireve for 1 rood of oats	$3\frac{1}{2}$d
From James le Blund for $\frac{1}{2}$ acre of oats	3d
Finstock	
From the Abbot of Eynsham for $2\frac{1}{2}$ acres & 1 rood of oats	$16\frac{1}{2}$d
From Adam Schort, Agnes Nod, Alice Sprot, Edward King, Cecilia Nod and Hugh Newman for 3 acres of oats	18d
From Richard of Hanborough for $\frac{1}{2}$ acre of winter wheat	6d
From Walter Aylward and John Leky for 1 rood of oats	$3\frac{1}{2}$d
From Edward King and Cecilia Nod for $1\frac{1}{2}$ roods of oats	9d
From William of Pachesdich, Elias Swein and Matilda Wylot for $1\frac{1}{2}$ acres of oats	9d
From Stephen of Hanborough for 1 rood of oats	$3\frac{1}{2}$d
North Leigh	
From the Abbot of Locus Sancti Edward for $\frac{1}{2}$ an acre of oats	3d
Tilgarsley	
From Peter carbonarius for $\frac{1}{2}$ an acre of winter wheat	6d
From Simon le Viiter for 1 acre of oats	6d
	From the Pleas of the Forest 1256

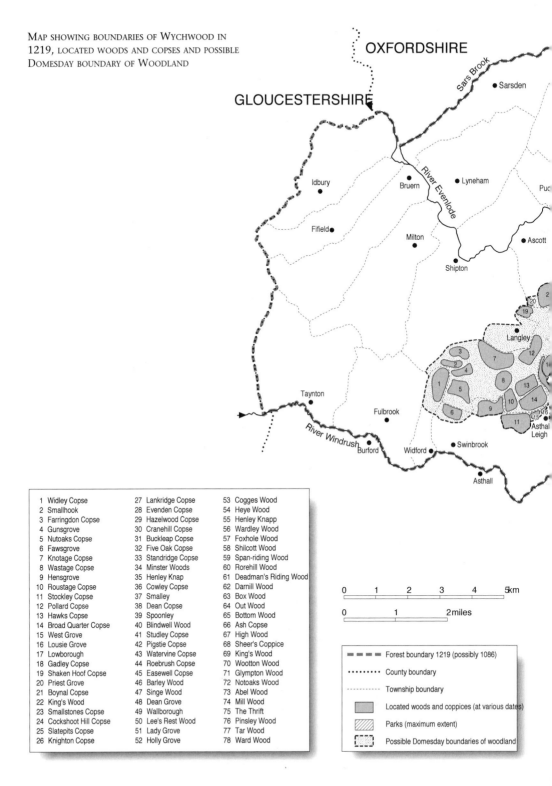

MAP SHOWING BOUNDARIES OF WYCHWOOD IN 1219, LOCATED WOODS AND COPSES AND POSSIBLE DOMESDAY BOUNDARY OF WOODLAND

1 Widley Copse	27 Lankridge Copse	53 Cogges Wood
2 Smallhook	28 Evenden Copse	54 Heye Wood
3 Farringdon Copse	29 Hazelwood Copse	55 Henley Knapp
4 Gunsgrove	30 Cranehill Copse	56 Wardley Wood
5 Nutoaks Copse	31 Buckleap Copse	57 Foxhole Wood
6 Fawsgrove	32 Five Oak Copse	58 Shilcott Wood
7 Knotage Copse	33 Standridge Copse	59 Span-riding Wood
8 Wastage Copse	34 Minster Woods	60 Rorehill Wood
9 Hensgrove	35 Henley Knap	61 Deadman's Riding Wood
10 Roustage Copse	36 Cowley Copse	62 Darnill Wood
11 Stockley Copse	37 Smalley	63 Box Wood
12 Pollard Copse	38 Dean Copse	64 Out Wood
13 Hawks Copse	39 Spoonley	65 Bottom Wood
14 Broad Quarter Copse	40 Blindwell Wood	66 Ash Copse
15 West Grove	41 Studley Copse	67 High Wood
16 Lousie Grove	42 Pigstie Copse	68 Sheer's Coppice
17 Lowborough	43 Watervine Copse	69 King's Wood
18 Gadley Copse	44 Roebrush Copse	70 Wootton Wood
19 Shaken Hoof Copse	45 Easewell Copse	71 Glympton Wood
20 Priest Grove	46 Barley Wood	72 Notoaks Wood
21 Boynal Copse	47 Singe Wood	73 Abel Wood
22 King's Wood	48 Dean Grove	74 Mill Wood
23 Smallstones Copse	49 Wallborough	75 The Thrift
24 Cockshoot Hill Copse	50 Lee's Rest Wood	76 Pinsley Wood
25 Slatepits Copse	51 Lady Grove	77 Tar Wood
26 Knighton Copse	52 Holly Grove	78 Ward Wood

Forest boundary 1219 (possibly 1086)

County boundary

Township boundary

Located woods and coppices (at various dates)

Parks (maximum extent)

Possible Domesday boundaries of woodland

20

THE MANAGEMENT OF THE FOREST

In the Middle Ages the Forest was administered by the Forester of Wychwood, who was from the fifteenth century sometimes called Keeper of Wychwood. This was an hereditary position. He was responsible for catching offenders who had broken the Forest law, either by hunting the deer or by interfering with their habitat – cutting down trees or underwood. (The poles produced by coppicing and pollarding, and the branches of trees felled for timber, are called 'underwood'. The more general term 'understorey' describes the vegetation found beneath the canopy of any woodland.) These offenders were brought first before the local court which was held by the Forester and those local freeholders who had been elected by the shire court to serve as verderers, that is judicial officers of the king's Forest. They imposed fines for lesser offences but all cases of venison (killing or hunting the deer) and more serious offences against the vert (the trees and underwood) were referred to the higher court, the Forest Eyre, which was held at intervals by the royal justices of the Forest. In the meantime the offenders were either imprisoned – there was a small prison at Langley – or put on bail. Mostly the punishment eventually imposed was a fine.

The Forester was also responsible for supplying the king with deer, wood, timber and charcoal when so ordered. These could be either for the king's own use or gifts to others. The Forester was answerable for his actions to the justices of the Forest, and the Forest could be taken away from the holder for any misuse of his authority. This happened on at least two occasions in Wychwood, when the Forest was returned to the Forester only on the payment of a large fine. From early in the thirteenth century the Forester lived at Langley.

There were also under-foresters, who assisted the Forester in his day-to-day duties, and other officials who helped in the management of the Forest and the enforcement of the Forest law. The chief of these were the verderers, elected by the shire court to assist the Forester in holding the preliminary trials of offenders in the Forest and in making a list of those offenders and offences which would be presented before the king's Forest justices when they visited the County. There were also agistors, who were chosen by the shire court to regulate the use of the woodland by pigs at specific times of the year, and to collect the income from this (known as pannage) and pass it on to the royal official. The third group of officials were the regarders, local freeholders who made an inspection of the Forest every three years, to detect any depredations against the vert, that is the woodland of the Forest. These depredations were waste (excessive cutting down of trees); assarting;

and purprestures (encroachments on Forest land for buildings and such like).

In addition, each of the private woods within the Forest had its own woodward, a man who worked for the lord of his manor, but who also had to answer to the Forester and to the justices of the Forest for any misdeeds within that wood – an invidious position.

The hierarchy of Forest officials altered over the centuries. In 1300 the under-foresters included a 'riding forester' as well as 'walking foresters'. From the fifteenth century there were two launders, who had the oversight of the two 'lawns' or clearings within the demesne woodlands, Ranger's Lawn and South Lawn. By the sixteenth century the western part of the Forest and purlieus was divided up into 'walks', each with its own keeper. There were five of these, each having a lodge within the woodland. At the end of the Forest's history these were located at High Lodge, Waterman's Lodge, South Lawn Lodge (or Burford Lawn Lodge), Brize's Lodge and Potter's Hill Lodge. There had earlier been another at Newell, but this is not recorded after 1591. There were actually two lodges at South Lawn, one, more prestigious, which was originally held by the man who was the launder and a smaller lodge which was used by the keeper. In addition there was Ranger's Lodge (formerly Shorthampton Lodge or Batten's Lodge) which acquired rather higher status around 1600. It was then the home of the man who had the day-to-day responsibility for the Forest, under its aristocratic keepers. Of these lodges, only Potter's Hill Lodge can be dated accurately. It was said to be newly built in 1591, by which time Newell Lodge, South Lawn (Burford Lawn) Lodge and Ranger's Lodge were already in existence. There was at least one more keeper's lodge in the purlieu woods, Capp's Lodge, but its occupant was a manorial, not a Forest, employee. There was probably a similar lodge at Whiteoak Green, where the keeper of Witney's woods lived.

The line of the de Langleys, the hereditary Foresters or keepers of Wychwood, died out in 1361 and the Forestership passed by descent or purchase to the Earls of Warwick and eventually, with the execution of Edward Earl of Warwick in 1499, into the hands of the Crown. After that date it was granted to a succession of holders for life, who were usually favoured courtiers. Among those who held the Forest in this way were Robert Dudley, the Earl of Leicester, Queen Elizabeth's favourite, and her Chancellor, Sir Thomas Fortescue. In 1661 Charles II granted Wychwood to his Chancellor, Lord Clarendon, and from him it passed by descent or purchase to the 4th Duke of Marlborough and his second son Lord Churchill.

They had an assistant, given different titles at different periods, who carried out most of the actual supervision of the Forest under these great lords. From the Tudor period onwards this post and some of the others in the Forest were occupied by men whom the king wished to reward. For example Henry VII appointed Anthony Fettiplace, his 'servant', as keeper of Cornbury Park and Launder of Burford Lawn and Thomas Crofte as Ranger of Wychwood – and in the last case the grant was said to be 'for service in the last victorious conflict', that is, the defeat of Richard III at Bosworth. By the end of the Tudor period the title of Ranger seems to have succeeded that of Forester.

The Forester's home at Langley was enlarged into a royal hunting lodge with a park by Henry VII, but it declined in importance because the various members of the gentry and nobility who were appointed as Lieutenants or Rangers of the Forest under the Tudor and Stuart monarchs also usually held the office of keeper of Cornbury Park, and administered the Forest from there. Cornbury was finally granted away by the crown in 1661. Woodstock Park, with the royal manors adjacent to it, was granted in 1705 to the 1st Duke of Marlborough. Langley and the demesne woodland remained as royal possessions.

In the later stages of the Forest's history its management became very complicated in that it was divided between three persons or government departments. The responsibility for the deer and the 'open' part of the Forest remained with the Ranger, the successor to the medieval Forester; but there were also coppices in the Forest, areas devoted to the production of timber and underwood, and the oversight of these was divided between the Department of Crown Lands, which was responsible for the underwood and leasing out of the coppices, and the Surveyor General of Woods who controlled the use of the timber. No one had overall control, with the result that there was a degree of mismanagement which is discussed later.

PARKS

A medieval park was a large enclosed area in which deer were kept. Royal permission was needed before a park could be created in the vicinity of a Forest. It was not necessarily woodland, and often included heath, grassland and even arable land, but woodland often lay at its heart. Although a distinct status symbol, medieval parks were often essentially deer farms. Gradually, and certainly by Tudor times, parks became appreciated for their attractive landscape, where huge ancient trees, sometimes pollarded, and ancient fossilised hedgerows were cherished.

Until the fourteenth century the only parks in the region belonged to the Crown and were at Cornbury and Woodstock, where the park

was extended to include land to the east of the River Glyme in stages Cornbury deer park
between probably the late twelfth and the fifteenth centuries or even
later. In 1329 John Wyard was given 'licence to empark' his small wood
at Stanton Harcourt, and in 1442 William Lovell was allowed to impark
his woods at Minster Lovell. Ditchley Park did not come into existence
until around 1600 and had originally been the residence of the keeper
of Bloxham Wood. Sir Henry Lee, Steward and Parker of Woodstock and
Ranger of the adjoining 'New Forest' for Queen Elizabeth I, began the
creation of the modern estate in which the park is situated.

THE LANDSCAPE OF THE FOREST

The earliest documentary evidence for the landscape is Domesday
Book, written in 1086, and it proves beyond doubt that a great deal of
the land within the bounds of the Forest was occupied by villages with
their arable fields and meadows. The manors in the western part of the
Forest and those in the south-east also included large amounts of
pasture. In Eynsham and Stanton Harcourt this may have been low-
lying flood-plain land, but in Churchill, Fifield, Fulbrook, Idbury,
Sarsden and Taynton this was almost certainly downland, such as still
existed in the nineteenth century.

However, the rest of the Forest consisted of woodland, mostly
belonging to the different manors in the region. The Domesday Book

entries suggest that these were scattered from Kidlington to Taynton, but actually the woods of Bloxham, Kidlington, Hensington, Sarsden and Taynton were detached from their manorial centres, and lay in the same area as the woods of the other manors and the royal woodland, forming a relatively compact block. Thus for example Shipton's woods were near Ramsden and Bloxham's near Charlbury. The only 'outliers' were Dean Grove in Dean, Pinsley Wood in Hanborough, and the woods in Stanton Harcourt. This meant that the whole of the extreme western part of the thirteenth-century Forest was devoid of anything that the men of the time would describe as a wood. It does not mean that there were no trees – hedgerow and other single trees would always have been valued assets. And there was a large heath in Fifield, Bruern and Milton, from which Bruern took its name (*brueria*, heath).

What was the woodland like? The medieval documents tell very little about this. Most of the evidence comes from the sixteenth century or later and may not necessarily apply to the earlier centuries. But it was definitely not an amorphous waste. With the possible exception of Faringdon Copse, which seems to have been shared by Taynton and Fulbrook, each of the manorial woods had well-marked boundaries, often defined by tracks or 'ways' through the woodland. Such 'ways' are found in the boundary clauses of four of the Saxon charters which survive for the area, for Witney manor in 969 and 1044, for Eynsham in 1005 and for Taynton in 1059, and more of these 'ways' defined the different parts of the Forest in 1300. Some of them are very old. Pay Lane which formed the boundary of the northern part of Witney manor in 969 is almost certainly a Roman road, whilst the 'mereway' (the Saltway from Stonesfield to Chipping Norton) which separated Fawler Wood and Bloxham Wood in 1300 is thought to be prehistoric in origin.

It is interesting to speculate as to how and when these manorial woods came into being. The earliest charter for the area is that of

Spelsbury, where the estates are called 'Hwiccewudu' in 840, but unfortunately it has no boundary clause which might have recorded wood. However the fact that it was a 10-hide estate both then and in 1086, when the manor included a large piece of woodland, suggests that the woodland of Wychwood was divided up between the manors even at that date. A hide, in this context, is an assessment for taxation purposes, with the number of hides indicating the relative size and wealth of the manor (although 'hide' is also used as a unit of area, approximately 120 acres). And the bounds of the northern, wooded, section of Witney manor in 969 are the same as the bounds of its two former hamlets of Hailey and Crawley today. In some cases it is tempting to see the woods as perhaps already being in existence in the Roman period – ancient woods indeed – with Widley Copse, Minster Woods and Asthall Woods belonging to the Roman villas and settlement in those parishes. On the other hand, in the Grim's Ditch area north of the Evenlode the Ditch seems only to correlate to the area of woodland itself, as if the land bounded by the ditch may have been allowed to go derelict and was divided up later. The parish boundaries there cross the Ditch, never follow it.

The large area of royal demesne woodland had not been attached to any manor, but it seems to have had a similar structure to the manorial

PAIN'S FARM, NEAR SWINBROOK, ONE OF THE LEAST CHANGED PARTS OF THE ANCIENT FOREST

27

woods. By the sixteenth century it was compartmented. Some areas, the coppices, were dedicated to growing trees and underwood; while the rest, the plains, were used principally as pasture both for the deer and for the animals of the people of the area. The coppices, too, were thrown open for pasture some of the time, and the whole of the woodland of the Forest was subject to common rights of grazing in this way, with one group of villages using the western section and another the eastern. After coppicing, the compartments of woodland would be fenced to protect the next generation of growth until it could survive grazing. There may well have been some ancient pollarded trees in the plains as well. The most similar surviving landscape of this kind is at Hatfield Forest, managed by the National Trust.

There is no definite evidence for the practice of coppicing in the royal demesne woods before the Tudor period, but some of the coppices described then are named in medieval documents and the shape of some of them fits so well into the pattern formed by some of the private woods, especially Knighton Copse and Loughborough Copse, that it seems very likely that they too existed earlier. Sales of (under)wood from the royal woodland are recorded in the thirteenth century, but usually only when the king had urgent need of money, not as a regular occurrence.

There were two clearings in the woodland, at Ranger's Lawn and Burford (or South) Lawn, and it is also probable that some of the 'open Forest' between the coppices was heath rather than dense woodland. That part of the Forest near Ramsden and Finstock was named as Ramsden Heath and Finstock Heath in a map of the Forest and purlieus made in 1815, and heaths are named in other areas: Baggs Heath formed part of Asthall's 'woodland'; while a 'Haethfeld' is recorded for Eynsham in 1005 and this heath extended into Hanborough and North Leigh. On the 1815 map the area to the north of Leafield and between Leafield and Langley is shown as clear of trees, and in 1791 this was said to be used as a sheepwalk.

The part of the Forest which lay between the Evenlode and the Glyme consisted of a number of manorial woods and the royal park at Woodstock, and here too it seems that there were some open areas among the wood. The boundary points recorded in the perambulations of the Forest of 1300 distinguish carefully between woods, fields (that is, common arable fields) and 'land', which is presumably open pasture, and some of this 'land' is found interspersed among the woods. A similar pattern of coppices with 'greens' between them is shown on nineteenth-century maps of the woods in the northern part of Crawley. The northern part of Hailey may have been similar, but most of that was assarted before the end of the thirteenth century, and assarts in Combe, Fawler and Finstock in the late thirteenth and early fourteenth centuries have similarly destroyed any evidence of the early structure of their woodland.

Because of these assarts, with smaller ones elsewhere, the amount of woodland in the Forest was considerably less in the mid-fourteenth century than it had been when Domesday Book was compiled, although it still provided 'Oxfordshire's leafiest landscape'. The impact of the Black Death on the region was so severe that there was little further clearance of the woods until the eighteenth and nineteenth centuries.

THE USE OF THE WOODLAND

The Bayeaux Tapestry shows us that at the time of William I woodland could be used for hunting, for warfare training and to stage social events of high status. More mundanely it could also be a source of revenue from fines. For the king, Wychwood was primarily a refuge for deer. For the lords and people of the manors in and around it, Wychwood was not only a place where their animals could be pastured but a source of structural timber and underwood which was essential for the upkeep of their houses and the making of the various implements and utensils needed for their daily life. The rights of housbote (for building timber) and heybote (for fencing material) still existed when the woods were in the Forest, but this timber and wood could only be taken from the woodland belonging to the manor and

COPPICE WITH STANDARD, STILL PRACTISED IN MODERN WYCHWOOD AND BENEFICIAL FOR WILDLIFE

30

only under the supervision of the Forester. If excessive use was made of a manorial wood, it could be taken away and kept temporarily or even permanently by the king – an early form of conservation management. The people of the Forest villages were almost certainly allowed to collect dead or fallen wood without any penalty and the people of Ramsden were still claiming this right in 1965!

In the Middle Ages the royal woods also functioned as a source of wood, timber and charcoal for the king, either for his own use or as gifts. Large amounts of timber were needed for the enlargement of the royal palace at Woodstock in the thirteenth century and this was supplied by the Forester or sometimes by the Bailiff of Woodstock Manor from the woods in and around the park. The Forester was also ordered to supply brushwood and charcoal when the king was expected at Woodstock. Many of the royal gifts were of firewood, sometimes to individuals but frequently to religious houses in Oxford and at Bruern, Burford and Coldnorton. Gifts of timber for building were also made to Oxford institutions, to Bruern Abbey locally and to Hailes Abbey and Lechlade Hospital in Gloucestershire amongst others.

The first evidence of exploitation of the manorial woods by coppicing comes only in the fourteenth century. It is possible that the woods had not been coppiced on any regular basis before that date, but it is also possible that coppicing is recorded then because there had been an alteration in the system of royal control. Instead of an infrequent eyre held by a Justice of the Forest at which forest offences from all over the county were reported and punished, more frequent inquisitions into the state of an individual Forest were held (again by a Justice of the Forest) and it is in their rolls that the coppicing is reported. Coppicing is an ancient practice, and it seems possible either that coppicing was not brought before the earlier eyres, or that the 'waste' recorded there was in fact coppicing.

The aim of coppicing was to produce a continuous crop of underwood, that is, poles of a more or less uniform length. To accomplish this an area of woodland was cut to the ground and then fenced for seven years, by which time the new growth was strong enough to withstand nibbling by the deer or other animals. In Wychwood, in the later stages of its history, the building and maintenance of this fencing was the responsibility of the Ranger, who was given the outermost 'acre' of the wood harvested at each felling which he could keep or sell when the fence was removed. In the coppices on the royal manors the tenant of the adjoining land had to build the fence and keep it in repair, and he also had the 'fence acre' at each felling. Coppicing produced crops of poles but in 1543 it was laid down by law that whenever a coppice was cut twelve trees were to be left per acre so that they could grow to provide timber.

There were twenty coppices in the royal demesne woodland (although this number varies because Lankridge Copse was sometimes divided into Great and Little Lankridge), giving a twenty-year cutting cycle. The boundary banks of some of them can still be detected in the surviving part of the forest. Other ephemeral coppices, for example Churchill and Fernhill Copses, appear in the records but they are not shown on the final definitive maps.

The larger private woods were also compartmented to provide coppices of a reasonable size. There were ten coppices in Crawley, three in the wood belonging to the manor of Shipton-under-Wychwood, three in Minster woods and eight in Spelsbury woods.

From the sixteenth century the royal coppices were leased out, often for life, to a private person and the crown received a rent for them. They were intended to be cut on a regular cycle, so that each year there would be one crop of wood, but the evidence shows that, in the seventeenth century at least, this rotation was not adhered to. This is not surprising since the coppices varied in size so that some would produce more income than others; and when a lease was due to expire there would be a temptation to get as much profit as possible in the time available. The coppices were inspected in 1617 by John Nordern, who reported that 'some of theis copices seeme to have bene felled out of their due course' and that it would be very difficult to get them back into the correct cycle. He also reported that there had been 'untimelie removing of the fenses' so that cattle and deer got in 'to the intollerable browsing and spoile of the woods'. Almost all of the coppices were either 'much spoyled by browsing' or contained 'much waste', which meant that their royal owner could not expect much revenue from them. Often the removal of the fences was deliberately done by local

OPPOSITE: THIS LATE FIFTEENTH-CENTURY FLEMISH ILLUSTRATION SHOWS HUNTING OF BOAR WITH DOGS, IN A 'COPPICE WITH STANDARD WOOD'. The foreground underwood has been felled recently, leaving scattered timber trees. In the background tall underwood awaits felling. Such areas were coppiced in rotation. After felling, the copse would be fenced to protect regrowth until it could survive grazing by deer and other livestock. Beyond lie pasture and dwellings. With the exception of the fantastic castle, it is comparable to the landscape at Pain's Farm, near Swinbrook, one of the least changed parts of ancient Wychwood (illustration page 27).

Information about wild animals is scarce, but wild boar were recorded in Wychwood in 1216. The earliest records of coppicing in Wychwood are from the fourteenth century. In England in 1543 it became law that when coppice was cut, twelve trees per acre – the 'standards' – should be left for timber. The system is co-incidentally beneficial for wildlife, and is still practised in Wychwood (illustration page 30).

We are indebted to Dr. Oliver Rackham for drawing our attention to this picture, which is reproduced by permission of the British Library and with the assistance of the Marc Fitch Fund.

34

men or even the Forest officials, to enable their cattle to get in and feed there. One occasion is reported when a heavy snowfall covered the fence and allowed deer to enter.

The located woods and copses of Wychwood are shown on the map on pages 20–21.

In 1791 there was a report to parliament on the state of the Forest. By then the coppices were being managed on a more regular cycle and it was the number of timber trees 'fit for the navy' that was of most importance to the government. In 1648 it had been laid down that the 'great trees, whereof the forest is full' were to be reserved for the navy but when Thomas Pride inspected the Forest in 1787 he wrote: 'I don't find the Government had any timber for the navy this century past – the produce has been appropriated chiefly to repairing the keepers' lodges'. In the 1791 report it was said that of the 27,600 oaks in the forest only 173 were fit for navy use, and there were more oaks in the open Forest than there were in the coppices, so clearly the rules regarding the preservation of standard trees had not been kept. The

WYCHWOOD FOREST 1791

Trees		Coppices	Open Forest
Oak	fit for navy	168	5
	20–50 years	5441	5774
	saplings < 20 years	2710	6880
	not improving	1141	5378
	firewood	69	37
	Total	*9529*	*18074*
Ash	improving	124	9882
	not improving	12	3012
	firewood	21	397
	Total	*157*	*13291*
Elm	improving	20	330
	not improving	–	2
	Total	*20*	*332*
Beech	improving	13	547
	not improving	1	13
	firewood	–	16
	Total	*14*	*576*
Sycamore	–	–	66
Lime		22	101
Horse chestnut		–	72

Reports of Crown Lands Vol 1, 1787–92. Tenth Report of the Commissioners Appointed to Enquire into the State & Condition of the Woods, Forests & Land Revenues of the Crown.

OPPOSITE: WILLIAM TURNER OF OXFORD (1789–1862), *A scene near where a pleasure fair was formerly held in Wychwood Forest*, 1809. The artist knew Wychwood, and the picture can be seen as a reflection on the passing of a local custom and a reference to the Forest as a place of retirement.

Reproduced by permission of the Victoria and Albert Museum, London, and with the assistance of the Marc Fitch Fund.

government was so concerned about this that it was suggested that someone should be appointed specifically to see that those rules were obeyed.

That report is the best indication of the vegetation of the Forest – oak and ash predominate with very little elm or beech. John Nordern's survey, in 1617, had reported the coppices as consisting mostly of hazel or thorn, but he was interested principally in the underwood and not the timber trees. The hazel would have been important as a source of fencing material and nuts, as well as fuel.

Although it was stated in the report that no timber had been cut for the navy for 100 years, there had been a little cut in 1788 and 1789, and there must have been more trees 'fit for navy use' than the report suggests.

Following the report the Commissioners for the Woods, Forests and Land Revenues of the Crown did employ a 'woodman' to be permanently in Wychwood, and a programme was begun of tidying up the Forest by cutting down and selling off all the 'dotard, decayed, unthrifty & shaken' trees, to leave room for younger ones to grow, followed by yearly cutting of timber for the navy, which was usually done in the coppice which was being cut that year and the open Forest near it. They also started to plant in the newly-felled coppices, at first acorns and later small trees – that is, to practise forestry in the modern sense. In view of what was to happen in the future all this activity seems rather pathetic – it would have taken one hundred years for the trees to grow to a usable size, by which time the navy no longer wanted wooden ships and the Forest itself had been disafforested and cleared. However, the commissioners were not to know that. And in the meantime, between 1807 and 1833, nearly three thousand loads of timber, probably the equivalent of some fifteen hundred trees, were taken from Wychwood, carried to Eynsham and there sent down the Thames to the Royal Dockyards, with the peak of activity occurring between between 1809 and 1812. Most of the timber was oak, although there was some ash and a small amount of beech. However, this was brought to an abrupt end in 1832, for a reason which is discussed later.

TIMBER SUPPLIED FOR THE NAVY 1803–33

Year	Oak		Ash		Beech	
	Loads	Feet	Loads	Feet	Loads	Feet
1803-6	nil					
1807	97	14	46	19	–	–
1808	74	6	73	2	–	–
1809	351	36			–	–
1810	265	25	26	41	15	4
1811	184	38	12	9	–	–
1812	273	39	–	–	21	44
1813	197	45	20	19	–	–
1814	–	–	24	15	–	–
1815	125	20	–	–	–	–
1816	88	16	–	–	–	–
1817	88	18	–	–	–	–
1818	78	40	–	–	–	–
1819	103	25	–	–	–	–
1820	79	23	–	–	–	–
1821	75	10	–	–	–	–
1822	83	–	–	–	–	–
1823	78	36	–	–	–	–
1824	86	35	–	–	–	–
1825	77	11	–	–	–	–
1826	84	35	–	–	–	–
1827	80	9	–	–	–	–
1828	69	9	–	–	–	–
1829	79	31	–	–	–	–
1830	91	13	–	–	–	–
1831	78	9	–	–	–	–
1832	53	9	–	–	–	–
1833	86	7	–	–	–	–

(A good 100-year-old tree was said to make 2 loads of timber)

ANIMALS IN THE FOREST WOODLANDS

The Forests were instituted for the protection of the deer, and care for their well-being was the first task of the Forester and his men. In the winter, when feed was scarce, branches were cut for browse-wood and hay was frequently bought for them. This is recorded as early as 1164.

Fallow deer are most often mentioned in the records, with red deer and roe deer being caught (legally or illegally) much less frequently. Red deer were the prime game, and were present at Domesday. Roe deer, also native, were less attractive as game and were no longer protected under the Forest law after 1338. Fallow deer, a Norman introduction coming originally from Persia via Sicily, were ideal for parks and poorer land. Venison was a status meat. The king gave not only venison, but also live deer to stock other parks, and occasionally deer-hunting rights to favoured subjects. These were gifts 'which money could not buy'.

Deer for the king's use was usually taken by the Forester or by royal huntsmen sent to Wychwood for that purpose. The venison was frequently salted, especially when it was to be sent to Westminster or, on one occasion, as far as York.

Records of the king hunting in person are scarce, presumably because there was no reason why this should have been noted down. The Bishop of Lincoln is recorded as having died whilst riding with the king (Henry I) in Woodstock Park in 1123, but they may not have been hunting at the time. The one king who is recorded as hunting in the

Wychwood area is James I – a poem describing this hunt can be found at Ditchley and is reproduced on page 46.

There are, however, some references to practices associated with a royal hunt. The owners of one estate in Bletchington are recorded from 1212 to 1376 as holding it on condition that they brought dinner, a roast of pork, to the king when he hunted in Cornbury, and in 1219 the holder of one piece of land in Milton (under Wychwood) had to bring a towel to wipe the king's hand when he hunted 'in the parts of Lankeleg' (Langley). In the twelfth century, at least, the villagers of the area must have had to assist at the king's hunt, because in 1110 the men of Eynsham were freed from that duty whenever the king's household was staying there.

Information about wild animals, apart from the deer, is hard to come by. There is a solitary reference to wild boar, in 1216. In the Middle Ages several men were granted permission to hunt (wild) cats, hares, badgers, and foxes. Birds too may have been hunted, especially woodcock. 'Cockshoot' occurs as a place-name twice in Wychwood, Cockshoothill Copse in the demesne forest and Cockshut Copse in Charlbury. A medieval cockshoot consisted of driving the birds into nets stretched between two adjoining areas of woodland.

From illuminated manuscripts showing medieval hunting scenes, the dogs used appear to have ranged from deer-hounds and mastiffs to small whippet-like greyhounds, and these are also found in the Forest records of Wychwood, sometimes being used illegally. Medieval French illustrations suggest that their kennels were elaborate buildings, but there is no medieval record of such in Wychwood. Possibly they were to be found at Langley, Cornbury or Woodstock Park, but on one occasion it is known that the king's huntsman brought his hounds with him and the king's bailiff at Woodstock was re-imbursed the money he had spent on their keep. Dog kennels are recorded in 1636 as having been built 'on the soil of the forest' by Acton Drake, then Ranger of the Forest, but this was said to be 'against the assize of the Forest' – that is, forbidden under Forest law. These were probably the dog kennels shown on later maps as adjoining the walls of Cornbury Park.

Grazing rights for animals in the woodland presumably preceded the Norman Forest. Domestic pigs were allowed into the Forest, in theory only between 14th September and 18th November each year and when there was sufficient 'mast' (acorns or beech-nuts). In the Middle Ages a fee called 'pannage' was charged for this. The system must have broken down in later centuries, as in 1791 it was said that 'the forest is over-run with swine'.

As we saw earlier, the villagers living in and around the woodland had the right to pasture other animals there, both in the royal and in the private woods. The existence of these rights of common was probably as great a factor as the Forest law in inhibiting the clearance of Forest land for agriculture, since in the Middle Ages any lord wishing to assart in his woodland had to reach an agreement with the lords of the other manors whose inhabitants had the right to common in those woods, as well as obtaining royal assent. These rights of common may have been for cattle and horses only, although goats were said to have been allowed in King John's reign. Sheep were usually said to be excluded from Forests but sheepwalks for Langley, Leafield, Shorthampton, Ascot, Asthall Leigh, Swinbrook, Fulbrook and Pain's Farm are recorded in the Report on the State of the Forest in 1791, and there are numerous other references to sheep in the wooded area north of the Evenlode.

THE PEOPLE AND SETTLEMENTS OF THE FOREST

The most important person in the Forest was, of course, the king. Some Forests were never visited by the king, being just a source of income. Wychwood however was a favourite haunt of most monarchs until the late seventeenth century. Apart from other attractions, it was a very convenient stopping-place when the king was journeying north-south or east-west through the kingdom. Henry III, in particular, continually enlarged and beautified his palace at Woodstock and, as already stated, Henry VII converted Langley into a royal hunting lodge. There is no record of the kings staying at Cornbury, the other royal park, after 1110 and it became used for a while as a stud for the king's horses. There was a lodge there in 1337, presumably the home of the 'parker', the man who was responsible for the park. This became much enlarged and was eventually re-built in the seventeenth century for Lord Danby, who held that office together with the keepership of the Forest, and for the Earl of Clarendon to whom Cornbury was granted by Charles II in 1661. As Chancellor from 1660 he was effectively head of the Government.

Until the eighteenth century the crown owned the manors around Woodstock (Hanborough, Combe, Stonesfield, Bladon and Wootton) and part of Bloxham Wood, as well as the royal parks. The crown's role as principal landowner of the Forest area was taken over, in the eighteenth and nineteenth centuries, by the Dukes of Marlborough. Woodstock manor and its hamlets were granted to the first Duke in 1705 by the crown. The derelict royal palace was destroyed and the new palace, Blenheim, was built within the park. Later dukes bought other manors in the vicinity as they became available and also acquired the keeping of the Forest and the lease of the coppices. The 4th duke and especially his younger son, the 1st Lord Churchill, to whom he bequeathed the Forest, had an inflated idea of their rights in it, claiming to own the deer and also the timber in the open parts, with the result that in 1832 there began a prolonged dispute with the Crown which had not been settled when Lord Churchill died in 1845. This prevented the felling of any timber trees for many years and may have postponed the enclosure of the Forest.

After the king, the most important people were those who owned the land within the Forest. In the Middle Ages the most prominent of these were ecclesiastics: the Bishop of Winchester who held Witney Manor, the Abbot of Eynsham who held Charlbury and acquired Finstock and Fawler as well as Eynsham itself, the Abbot of Winchcombe who held Enstone, the Abbot of Netley who owned North Leigh and the Prior of Deerhurst who held Taynton. The Abbot of Eynsham was the only one who lived in the area. The other estates would all have been administered by stewards.

As well as owning these manors, monasteries had, by the thirteenth century, become responsible for four hermitages which were once located in the woodland of Wychwood. In some cases it is not known how and when these originated, but King John is said to have appointed two chaplains to celebrate divine service at the hermitage at Ewelme (Newhill). This was in the care of Bruern Abbey. The hermitage at Felley (Phelleley), which was located in Bloxham Wood on a site now within Ditchley estate, was older. By about 1145 it belonged to Eynsham Abbey, although it was still called a hermitage. The other hermitages were at Lovebury, which was originally held by a single hermit but in 1270 was given into the care of the Hospital of St John the Baptist at Lechlade, and Lockslegh which belonged to the Priory of Deerhurst and was located in the woods belonging to Deerhurst's manor at Taynton. Although these hermitages were within the woodland, they were not completely isolated since they lay on the routes which would have been used by travellers and those whose work took them there; and they did have a purpose apart from the hermit's possible desire for a solitary life. In 1364 it was the Forester of Wychwood who complained that the prior of the Hospital of St John at Lechlade had not provide anyone to live at Lovebury, saying that his men, who spent most of their time moving around in the Forest, needed to be able to hear mass.

After the dissolution of the monasteries between 1536 and 1539, these estates, with the exception of Witney, passed into the hands of lay owners.

Of the lay lords the most important in the Middle Ages was the Earl of Gloucester, who owned Shipton-under-Wychwood and its hamlets as well as Burford, just outside the Forest. The Earls of Warwick held Spelsbury. However, these men were rarely resident on their manors. Both of these estates had come into the possession of the crown by the end of the fifteenth century, and were later held by men of the gentry class.

At the other end of the social scale from the Dukes of Marlborough were the inhabitants of the Forest village of Leafield, which was entirely surrounded by the woodland and had very little agricultural land. Although in 1552 this had been divided between several inhabitants, each with a few acres, by 1839 the greater part of it was in three farms and two small holdings, with most of the remaining village men having less than a rood of land (a quarter of an acre) each. Many had only a cottage, a garden and a pigsty, and the final maps of Wychwood which were made around that date show a number of tiny encroachments, presumably pigsties, on the Forest land around the village. Similar small encroachments were found around Ramsden which, although not surrounded by woodland like Leafield, was on the edge of it. In Leafield's case it is not surprising to find that in the census of 1851 more than a third of the men there are said to be earning their living in the woodland, as woodmen, wood labourers, sawyers, hurdle-makers, or game-keepers.

In the Middle Ages there were other Forest hamlets like Leafield, although smaller, which have now disappeared completely: Slape, in Wootton parish; and Boriens, in Glympton. Many of their inhabitants are named in the Forest pleas of the thirteenth century for offences against the vert.

Those records also accuse the inhabitants of all the villages in and around the woodland of:

> having a cart with which he enters both the demesne woods of the Lord King and others having woods in the forest, and takes away wood both from the high wood and the underwood, and he takes wood for fencing with which to enclose his corn, and when the same corn is carried away he is accustomed to take the fencing to

Oxford or other markets around, for sale, together with other wood which he takes in the aforesaid woods both by day and night, either himself or through his servants. So that... each one of them has every week two cartloads of wood at least from the aforesaid forest to its great destruction... Besides there are in the same villages countless cottagers continually going into the aforesaid woods and taking away an infinite number of bundles of branches and underwood to the great destruction of the forest.

The same complaint about the plundering of the woodland by the local villagers was made in the 1791 Report on Wychwood and in another report in 1848. Perhaps it is surprising that any woodland remained at the end of its seven hundred years as a Royal Forest.

BIBLIOGRAPHY

On Wychwood
Kibble, John, *Wychwood Forest and its Border Places*, 1999 (2nd edn.), The Wychwood Press.
Schumer, Beryl, *Wychwood: the Evolution of a Wooded Landscape*, 1999, The Wychwood Press.
Watney, Vernon J., *Cornbury and the Forest of Wychwood*, 1910, privately published.

On Forests in general:
Grant, Raymond, *The Royal Forests of England*, 1991, Alan Sutton.
James, N. D. G., *A History of English Forestry*, 1981, Basil Blackwell.
Young, Charles R., *The Royal Forests of Medieval England*, 1979, Leicester University Press.

On other Forests:
Hawkins, Desmond, *Cranborne Chase*, 1980, Victor Gollancz.
Macdermott, Edward T., *A History of the Forest of Exmoor*, 1973 (rev. edn), David & Charles.
Rackham, Oliver, *The Last Forest: The History of Hatfield Forest*, 1989, J. M. Dent.
Steel, David, *The Natural History of a Royal Forest* [Shotover], 1984, Pisces Publications, Oxford.

On woodland:
Rackham, Oliver, *Hayley Wood, its History and Ecology*, 1975, Cambs & Isle of Ely Naturalists Trust.
Rackham, Oliver, *Trees and Woodlands in the British Landscape*,1976, J. M. Dent.
Rackham, Oliver, *Ancient Woodland: its History, Vegetation and Uses in England*, 1980, Edward Arnold.

Some royal sporting snippets

Edward, second Duke of York, wrote 'Hunting and the Master of the Game' between 1406 and 1413, at a time when a more chivalrous approach to hunting was becoming fashionable. His book owes much to the famous French feudal lord, Count Gaston de Foix, who died in 1391. Edward married the widow of a Keeper of Wychwood. She held Langley Manor, and Edward may have hunted in Wychwood. These extracts are taken from a rendering of his work contained in the Wickham Steed papers held at the Centre for Oxfordshire Studies.

The harts be the swiftest beasts and strongest and of marvellous great cunning... Men take them with hounds, with greyhounds and with nets and cords, and with other harriers, with pits and with shot [*i.e. a bow*] and with other gins and with strength. But in England they are not slain except with hounds or with shot or with strength of running hounds.

◆ ◆ ◆ ◆ ◆

A hound is of great understanding and of great knowledge, a hound hath great strength and great goodness, a hound is a wise beast... The greatest fault of hounds is that they live not long enough.

◆ ◆ ◆ ◆ ◆

A good greyhound should go so fast that if he be well slipped he should overtake any beast, and there where he overtakes it he should seize it... He should be good and kindly and clean, glad and joyful and playful, well willing and goodly to all manner of folks save to the wild beasts to whom he should be fierce, spiteful and eager.

◆ ◆ ◆ ◆ ◆

The mastiff's nature and his office is to keep his master's house, and it is a good kind of hound, for they keep and defend with all their power all their master's goods. They be of churlish nature and ugly shape.

◆ ◆ ◆ ◆ ◆

And since hunters eat little and sweat always they should live long and in health. Wherefore I counsel to all manner of folk of what estate or condition they be, that they love hounds and hunting.

◆ ◆ ◆ ◆ ◆

The forester well ought to know of his great deer's haunts. He shall lead the hunter and the lymerer [*holder of hounds on a leash*] thither without noise... and then ought the lymerer by bidding of the hunter to cast round with the lymer the quarter that the deer is in, and set all the covert to know whether he is gone away or abides there still. [*To 'set the covert' was to go round the covert, looking carefully for any sign that the hart had left the place.*] If he abides, then shall the lymerer go where the hart went in... and break a bough of green leaves and lay it where the hart went in and then draw fast to the meeting...

◆ ◆ ◆ ◆ ◆

One chapter is entitled 'Of the Ordinance and the Manner of Hunting when the King will hunt in Forests or in Parks for the Hart with bows and greyhounds and stable'.

The Master of the Game should be in accordance with the master forester or parker where it should be that the King should hunt that day, and if the tract be wide, the forester should warn the sheriff of the shire for to order sufficient stable [*men and hounds to place at various points*], and carts also to bring the deer that should be slain to the place where the curees [*probably the 'gralloching' or disembowelling of the quarry*] at hunting have usually been held... and the forester should have men ready there to meet them, that they go no farther, nor straggle about for fear of frightening the game before the King comes. If the hunting shall be in a park, all men should remain at the park gate, save the stable that ought to be set ere the King comes...

Early in the morning the Master of the Game should be at the wood to see that all be ready, and he or his lieutenant or such hunters as he wishes, ought to set the greyhounds, and whoso be teasers [*hounds to tease out or put up the game*] to the King or Queen, or to be their attendants. As often as any hart cometh out he should when he passes blow a mote [*sound the horn*] and recheat [*call together the hounds, to begin or continue the chase*], and let slip to tease it forth... then the master forester or parker ought to show him the King's standing if the King would stand at his bow, and where all the remnants of the bows would stand. And the yeoman of the King's bows ought to be there to keep and make the King's standing, and remain there without noise till the King comes. And the grooms that keep the King's dogs and broken greyhounds should be there with him, and also the Master of the Game should be informed by the forester or parker what game the King should find within the set.

Then should the Master of the Game mount upon his horse and meet the King and bring him to the standing and tell him what game is within the set, and how the greyhounds be set, and also the stable, and also tell him where it is best for him to stand with his bow or with his greyhounds, for it is to be known that the attendants of his chamber and of the Queen's should be best placed, and the two fewterers [*keeper of greyhounds*] ought to make fair lodges of green boughs at the tryste [*the appointed station for the hunt*] to keep the King and Queen and ladies and gentlewomen and also the greyhounds from the sun and bad weather.

When the King is at his standing, and the Master of the Game has set the bows and assigned who shall lead the Queen to her tryste, then he should blow for the uncoupling; the hart-hounds and the harriers that before have been led by some forester thither where they should uncouple, and all the hounds that belong to both mutes [*packs*] waiting for the Master of the Game's blowing... then should the harrier uncouple his hounds and blow three motes and seek forth. And as oft as he passes within the set from one quarter to another, he should blow drawing... And after the harriers have well run and well made the rascal void [*caused the small deer to leave the covert*], then should the sergeant and the berners [*hound handlers*] of the hart hounds blow three motes, and uncouple there where they suppose the best ligging [*lair*] is for a hart... If the hart goes to the greyhounds and if it goes to the bows, he should take up his hounds and reward them a little, and if the hart escapes out of the set, he should take them and go again to the wood and look if he may meet with anything. And one thing is to be known, that the hart hounds should never be uncoupled before any other, unless a hart be readily harboured... or else that they may be in a park...

And all the while the hunting lasteth should the carts go about from place to place for to bring the deer to the curee. And there should be the server of the hall... to lay the game in a row, all the heads one way, and every deer's to the other's back...

And when the covert is well hunted and cleared, then should the Master of Game come to the King to know if he would hunt any more... If the King will hunt no more, then should the Master of Game, if the King will not blow, blow a mote... Then should the Master of Game lead the King to the curee, and show it to him. And then the King shall tell the Master of Game what deer he should ware [*give away*] and to whom, and if the King wishes to stay, he may; nevertheless he usually goes home when he hath done this.

James I hunted in Wychwood in 1608 and 1610, and his exploits are commemorated at Ditchley Park by the following doggerel verses which accompany the antlers of six hunted harts. Several of the 'points', individual chases, described were quite a distance, for example on 25th August 1610 from Foxhole Wood north-west of Ditchley to the heart of Woodstock Park, near the bridge at modern Blenheim.

SATURDAY 24TH AUGUST 1608

From Foxhole Coppice rouz'd
Great Brittain's King I fled
But what; in Kiddington Pond
He overtook me dead.

MONDAY 26TH AUGUST 1608

King James made me to run
For life from Dead Mans Riding.
I ran to Goreil Gate,
Where death for me was biding.

TUESDAY 27TH AUGUST 1608

The King pursude me fast,
Fast fro' Grange Coppice flying.
The King did hunt me me living,
The Queen's Parke had me dying.

WEDNESDAY 22ND AUGUST 1610

In Henly Knap to hunt me
King James, Prince Henry found me.
Cornbury Park River,
To end their hunting, drowned me.

FRIDAY 24TH AUGUST 1610

The King and Prince from Grange,
Made me to make my race,
But death neere Queenes Parke
Gave me a resting place.

SATURDAY 25TH AUGUST 1610

From Foxehole driven,
What could I doe,
Being lame I fell
Before the King and Prince
Neere Rozamond her Well.

Wychwood Forest transformed: the Forest in the nineteenth century

KATE TILLER

The act to disafforest and enclose Wychwood was passed in 1853. This precisely fixed legal event is easy to identify, as are the transformations which followed it. Less immediately apparent, but also of great importance, are the transformations in custom and culture, in social relations, in economic activities and in natural ecology which may have preceded or succeeded disafforestation and enclosure. It is on these varied but frequently interrelated aspects of Wychwood's history in the eighteenth and nineteenth centuries that this chapter will concentrate.

THE FOREST AT THE BEGINNING OF THE NINETEENTH CENTURY

As Beryl Schumer has shown, the legal bounds and physical extent of Wychwood have varied at different periods. In the eighteenth and nineteenth centuries the perambulation of the Forest followed the

WYCHWOOD IN THE EARLY NINETEENTH CENTURY

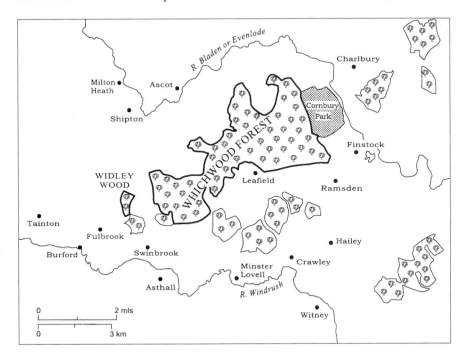

Wychwood Forest as shown on the first
edition of the one-inch Ordnance Survey map
of England and Wales, 1833, with the
railway added later

boundaries shown in the map on page 47. It encompassed 3750 acres, roughly equally divided between coppice and open Forest. Beyond that were the purlieu woods, whose inhabitants had commoning rights in the Forest and where the forestal rights of herbage or feed for the King's deer also applied. These purlieu areas were generally parts of the old royal Forest previously disafforested, either by grant or trespass.

The Forest was used in three main ways: for deer, for the production of wood and for common grazing. Some timber from Wychwood was used for naval shipbuilding. Woodland was managed as coppices with standards. Between 1596 and 1831 common practice was for coppices to be leased, typically to the Forest Ranger. The reduced interest of the crown in the direct management of the Forest was a recurrent theme in this period. As to grazing, seventeen places had rights of common pasture in Wychwood. How these common rights were defined is a vital part of understanding how the Forest changed in the eighteenth and nineteenth centuries. These three uses – deer, timber and common grazing – could be kept in sustainable equilibrium in a wood-pasture regime if the natural ecology was effectively managed. This is the clear view of Michael Freeman in his recent work on the environmental history of Wychwood, which is further discussed below. In such a sustainable regime the deer are contained in open Forest areas, coppiced woodland protected, the understorey controlled by grazing and cropping, in a cycle of annual feed and fuelling. Was this the case with Wychwood?

Arthur Young remains a valuable, if contentious, observer of Wychwood at the start of the nineteenth century. He visited in 1807, riding sixteen or seventeen miles to form a direct impression of the Forest. His account was published in *A General View of the Agriculture of Oxfordshire (1809 and 1813)*. As a proponent of agricultural improvement, Young describes, judges and prescribes solutions to what he discerns to be the problems of Wychwood. He lists the common rights – for horses and sheep only. No cattle or hogs should be commoned in the Forest, but many were there 'by trespass' – an early indication of the gulf between theory and practice of the use of the Forest, or perhaps between contending views of exactly what was customary.

Young notes the thirty-four copses of Wychwood; the soils – 'reddish good loam or the common stonebrash'; and the trees – oak, ash and beech, with some standard oaks 60–70 years old but not yet of use for the navy. He noted also the understorey growth of the open Forest; hawthorn, hazel and field maple were the typical species. He is dismissive of the standard timber – 'when these trees are compared with the space of the land in which they are found, they cease to be an object of any consideration'. As for the open Forest this 'produces nothing, but a certain quantity of brush-fuel, and browse for the deer'.

By the time Young was writing, perceptions of forest landscapes had been influenced by notions of the picturesque. Young acknowledges the aesthetic appeal of Wychwood – 'I found many very beautiful scenes, particularly where the nut fair is held, a glen by Mr Dacre's lodge... there are vales, also, of the finest turf. Several of these scenes want nothing but water to form most pleasing and finished landscapes'. But these sensibilities must in Young's view be overridden by the need for improvement, i.e. enclosure, to realise the productive potential of Wychwood.

The present 'agreeable circumstances' for local people might delay from happening what 'ought for a 1000 reasons, to take place as soon as possible... the object is hereby to make a large tract of good land productive to the public... this would take place on it being made private property, in whatever hands it might be placed... there are no circumstances (the mere pleasure of wandering alone excepted) which may not be fully compensated, by the solid and valuable considerations of allotments'. Young seems to see no contradiction in realising the public good by creating private property. Nor does he confine himself to considerations of economic productivity or aesthetics when anatomising Wychwood. Enclosure was essential because of 'the morals of the whole surrounding county demand it imperiously'. He pictures in effect a dependency culture in the villages around the Forest which 'have or usurp a right of commonage'. This would have included Finstock, Ramsden, Hailey, Crawley, Minster Lovell, Asthall, Swinbrook, Leafield, Shipton, Milton and Ascott. The full force of his moral judgements for enclosure of the Forest comes over in a much-quoted passage:

The vicinity is filled with poachers, deerstealers, thieves, and pilferers of every kind; offences of almost every description abound so much, that the offenders are a terror to all quiet and well-disposed persons; Oxford gaol would be uninhabited were it not for this fertile source of crimes. This is a consideration that will surely have its weight with every man who sees the evil, and must consequently wish for the only remedy the case admits. [That is, to enclose Wychwood.]

A similarly mixed picture of the past emerges from Charles Belcher's essay *On reclaiming of Wastelands as instanced in Whichwood Forest* (1863). It was 'unreclaimed forest land, dense, dark and gloomy; its silence seldom disturbed, except by the axe of the woodman, the gun of the gamekeeper, or the stealthy tread of the deerstealer'.

The painting of Wychwood in 1809 by William Turner of Oxford (1789–1862), on page 34, also has limited tranquillity. He titles it a 'scene near where a pleasure fair was formerly held in Wychwood Forest'. The original is in the Victoria and Albert Museum and was exhibited in the Oxfordshire County Museum in 1984 during a major travelling exhibition of Turner's work. The artist knew Wychwood and the exhibition catalogue suggests that there is in this picture a sense of identification with place, a musing on the passing of a local custom (the fair), and a reference to the Forest as a place of retirement and meditation, yet here appearing far from tranquil. The writhing trees and calling horse produce a composition apparently based on Titian's painting *St Peter Martyr* (the trees following the struggling figures of the saint and his assassin) and represent a turmoil appropriate to the threat of enclosure.

Let us return to the historian's view of Wychwood before and after enclosure. There has been a great deal of recent work on Forests and Wychwood in particular, including that of E. P. Thompson, Michael Freeman, the late Frank Emery, myself, and Mark Hathaway. I will now draw on that work and on the voices of some who were there.

E. P. Thompson, in his study of 'Custom, law and common right' (1991), saw Forests as 'notable arenas, in the eighteenth century, of conflicting claims (and appropriations) of common rights'. The Forest courts (and with them direct Crown 'invigilation') were in decline. Royal Forests became something of a free for all. In Thompson's words,

> The hierarchy of grantees, managers, keepers, forest officers, under-keepers, remained in being, as avaricious as ever, and most of them engaged in the rip-offs which their rank or opportunities of office favoured. The great encroached on the walks, fenced in new hunting lodges, felled acres of timber or obtained little sweeteners... In the middle of the hierarchy forest officers and under-keepers, who had long supplemented their petty salaries with perquisites, made in-roads into the venison, sold off the brushwood and furze, made private agreements with innkeepers and pastry-cooks, butchers and tanners.

It is a vivid picture and one which is borne out by Thompson's quotation from Charles Withers, the Surveyor General for Woods and Forests, who kept a diary of a tour of some of the royal Forests in the 1720s and who wrote of Wychwood:

This forest egregiously abused. The timber shrouded and browsed: none coming on in the Knipes or Coppices; cut by Keepers without assignment, sold to the neighbourhood, especially in Burford Town supplied thence. Landlord Nash at the Bull [the inn on the hill in Burford] bought this year ten load; in short 'tis scandalous.

Thompson in his study of Windsor Forest and Douglas Hay on Cannock Chase have considered these eighteenth-century Forests as settings for the assertion of continuing customs in common, and of battles between government and governed over the definition and presentation of those customs. A feature of these battles they define as 'social crime', that is actions criminal to the law and its enforcers; but from the local perspective they were a matter of communally supported social protest, directed at particular individuals or groups. Michael Freeman has taken up some of these themes, using evidence from Wychwood in the eighteenth and nineteenth centuries, particularly deer stealing, wood stealing, natural ecology and social relationships. He draws a convincing picture of an environment under great pressure as more and more people tried to exploit it to the full; 'All parties strove to exercise their own advantages, the common people as much as the rich or the middling sort'. Thus, with decline in royal influence, the Forest bureaucrats sought to extend their own rights (from the Royal Ranger down).

For the local villagers too the opportunities were irresistible – 'the open forest and the open heathlands around it offered a harvest to even the most land-poor amongst the commoning population... the forest and its wastes became an island of commonage in a steadily expanding sea of holdings in severalty. It became a magnet for the landless...' A combination of activities – stock keeping (with common grazing rights), pottery at Leafield, outworking in the woollen and gloving industries, quarrying and lime burning – combined to sustain Forest and purlieu dwellers in a period of growth in population. In 1791 the Board of Land Revenue reported that 'the Forest was illegally overrun with swine in the coppices as well as in the general wastes'. Not just dead and snap wood was being taken but bushes were being cut and young trees lopped. Local people were exploiting Wychwood's natural resources to an unprecedented degree. Other pressures came from the Crown, particularly in wartime periods when timber for naval building was needed. (In 1792, for example, this produced an income for Wychwood of £1566 2s 3d as against expenditure of £395 3s 3d.) Even the deer were increasing in numbers to around 1,000 fallow deer in 1792. By 1847–8 this had apparently risen to 1,500 or 1,600.

The combination of these pressures on the Forest together with a collapse in management of its resources resulted, in Freeman's view, in a degradation of the natural environment. The ecosystem of a carefully balanced wood-pasture environment was undermined. This deterioration followed overgrazing – sheep, oxen, pigs, deer and rabbits all played a part. The legacy of degraded soils, leached and non-calcareous, was to have its effect when areas of Wychwood were turned into arable land at disafforestation, a point to which we shall return.

The consequences of the eighteenth-century Forest regime, or lack of it, were not only environmental. Freeman considers also the social relationships and customs of eighteenth-century Wychwood. Evidence on deer stealing, potentially a 'social crime', as defined by Thompson and Hay, is provided by the Quarter Sessions and Cornbury Estate papers. Some 300 incidents of deer stealing are recorded between 1760 and 1830. The names of the offenders, their abode, occupation and details of their crimes can be analysed. All came from West Oxfordshire and East Gloucestershire. The great majority of the perpetrators came from rural communities, although some were from Burford and Witney. A majority were labourers but there were some named craftsmen and tradesmen. There seem to have been kinship links, particularly in the eighteenth century, and deer stealers on occasion went round in gangs. Their target was obviously the deer, although there were instances of physical violence against named individuals, particularly when pressure of prosecution was strongest. Freeman concludes that this violence was not particularly directed against the Crown, which was absentee in its influence, nor against the main Forest offices; indeed he points to examples of paternalism on the part of the Forest rangers. Neither were the keepers targeted, although they did fall foul on occasion. There was a nasty episode in which two of the dogs of a keeper were kidnapped and found hung up on a tree in the Forest. A majority of deer stealers were young men in their late teens and early twenties, which leads perhaps to another interpretation of this behaviour.

On occasion deer stealing seems to have been for venison sales to butchers and innkeepers. Sometimes it was an occasional pursuit of village craftsmen or labourers, 'whether to exact some test of male virility' or 'for the domestic pot'. What there was in common was the tendency to give legitimacy to such behaviour by claiming it was the exercise of a customary right. This use of custom as a cloak of respectability was a tactic employed across the social spectrum by those exploiting the Forests. If there was social unrest in Wychwood villages it was less between rich and poor as 'between the poor and... small-time peasant farmers and proprietors' who by the 1790s were having to cope with increasing poverty (and therefore poor rate payments) and the emerging effects of ecological stress. Given the range of people benefiting or hoping to benefit from the loosened customary regime of Wychwood it is not surprising that, as Arthur Young agreed, there was extreme resistance to 'improvement' by enclosure.

CHANGES TO THE FOREST

How did the Forest eventually change? One way was in response to the moral onslaught expressed by many others as well as Young. The annual feasts and festivals which 'celebrated and reaffirmed the bounty that the Forest offered to its inhabitants' were, as research by Mark Hathaway demonstrates, a particular target in the first half of the nineteenth century. There were three main events of this kind, all of which had ceased by 1856 and the enclosure of the Forest.

The Whitsun Feast, held at Capp's Lodge, north-east of Burford, was abandoned in 1827 under the influence of an evangelical curate concerned about 'gross improprieties'. It was replaced by an event in Burford town hall, attended by local gentry and tradespeople who feasted on venison provided by the then Forest Ranger, the 1st Lord Churchill.

The Whit Hunt in Chase Wood, near Crawley, north of Witney, was associated with fights between rival villages, drinking, music, morris dancing and the eating of venison, for up to six days. Dogs and huntsmen were supplied by Lord Churchill, as Forest Ranger, until 1835 and thereafter by the Heythrop Hunt. The Whit Hunt ceased in 1850.

Then there was the Wychwood Forest Fair. This apparently began in 1796 as a nonconformist event, countering the 'disorder' of other fairs. It was held in the third week of September, following St Giles' Fair in Oxford and Witney Feast in the first and second weeks of the month respectively. It attracted large numbers of stallholders. By 1810, ten thousand people were said to be attending. The fair was overseen by the Forest Ranger's staff with additional special constables being sworn in. Tensions between post-harvest jollification and fears of 'idle and disorderly characters' were a recurring feature. The fair was barred in 1831, 1832, 1833, 1843 and 1845, all years of some political unrest. At other times Lord Churchill, his family and other gentry attended the fair, held on Newhill Plain. The Yeomanry Band played and ever increasing numbers of people came to Wychwood. In 1846 it was claimed 20,000 were there; in 1853 (the first year of the Oxford,

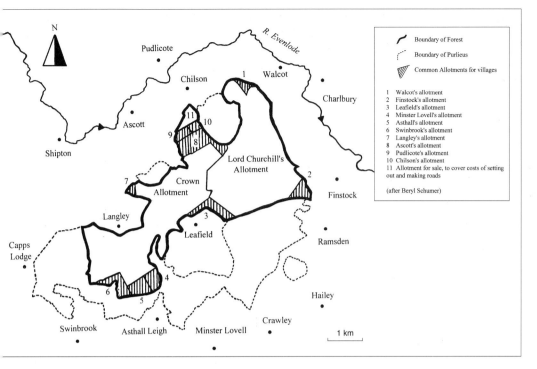

N

Pudlicote •

R. Evenlode

Chilson •

Walcot •

1

Charlbury •

Ascott •

11 10

9

8

Shipton •

Lord Churchill's
Allotment

2

7

Crown
Allotment

Finstock •

Langley •

3

Leafield •

Ramsden •

Capps
Lodge •

6

5

4

Hailey •

Swinbrook •

Asthall Leigh •

Minster Lovell •

Crawley •

1 km

Boundary of Forest

Boundary of Purlieus

Common Allotments for villages

1   Walcot's allotment
2   Finstock's allotment
3   Leafield's allotment
4   Minster Lovell's allotment
5   Asthall's allotment
6   Swinbrook's allotment
7   Langley's allotment
8   Ascott's allotment
9   Pudlicote's allotment
10 Chilson's allotment
11 Allotment for sale, to cover costs of setting
    out and making roads

(after Beryl Schumer)

Worcester and Wolverhampton Railway) it was 50,000. But these were to be the last years of the fair which ended in 1856. Lord Churchill, as Forest Ranger, felt compelled to abandon it because of drunkenness and debauchery. He had trenches dug across the fair ground, just as the disafforestation and enclosure of Wychwood, so eagerly championed by Arthur Young, was finally under way.

To read accounts of this most marked of changes is to hear the full self-confidence of Victorian 'high farming' loud and clear. A strong economy, a growing home market as yet largely untouched by the threat of imported goods, and technical advances (in drainage, machinery, the application of steam power, farm buildings and their layout, and the production of artificial fertilisers) all contributed to a resurgence of agricultural improvement and specifically of enclosure activity.

For Wychwood this meant the creation of 2,937 acres as a Crown allotment, of which about 1,970 acres were reclaimed Forest land. Around 1,700 acres were retained by the second Lord Churchill in lieu of his now lost office as Forest Ranger. There was therefore some remaining wooded area, but it was in the 1,970 acres cleared for arable from Forest that the most dramatic changes were immediately seen. The picture is painted by C. Belcher, a farmer of Little Coxwell, near

ALLOTMENTS MADE AT
THE DISAFFORESTATION
OF WYCHWOOD

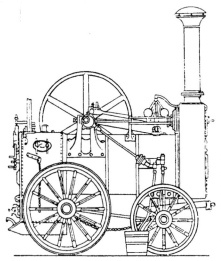

A PORTABLE ENGINE OF 1853, FROM WHICH THE FIRST TRACTION-ENGINES DEVELOPED

Faringdon, writing in a prize essay of 1863. Belcher records that seven new farms, Ascott, High Lodge, Fairspear, Leafield, Potters Hill, Langley and South Lawn were created from 'unreclaimed forest land'. First the deer were cleared (mostly killed), then hundreds of men and boys ('such an army... as might have been looked on with pleasure, even by a member of the Peace Society') cleared the brushwood. Next large trees were uprooted (with the aid of Fowler's tree-throwing machine) or felled and the roots grubbed up and burnt. Fences were put up, ten miles of new roads built, water supplied and new farmhouses and farmsteads erected. All this mighty labour was achieved between October 1856 and January 1858, a period of sixteen months. The seven farms were advertised in 1858 on thirty-one year leases and Belcher, who became tenant of Potters Hill Farm, north of Asthall, recalls sowing the first 'forest' crops in the spring of 1858. He acknowledges that the land was difficult to work with remaining roots, brambles and fern-stems. This problem he tackled by having the 320 acres to be planted with oats breast-ploughed, then harrowed by horses, a method he repeated in subsequent years.

Belcher's quest to win productive land from the Forest appears as one of truly Victorian heroic proportions. He launches his account in suitably biblical terms, answering 'the first supreme command to man, "Replenish the earth and subdue it"'. His estimation of the results is similarly redolent of the period. The 'new' Wychwood affords 'honest employment to the horny hands of those who toil early and late for their daily bread', and has transformed the morality of the Forest area from the bad old days of 'poachers, idlers and thieves' of dissipation, transportation and neglect of family. Above all Belcher's picture of Wychwood is one of success and of progress, in an age where the ingenuity of man no longer permits the existence of waste.

This buoyant note was maintained by the Land Surveyors' Club, whose visit to Wychwood was reported in *The Times* in July 1859. The Land Surveyors' Club, 'which comprises gentlemen from every part of England', did indeed inspect 'this great work'. On 13 July 1859 they were invited by John Clutton, who went over the ground with them. He was the surveyor who had been appointed (along with the Commissioners, under the original disafforestation act of 1853) to estimate the rights of the Crown. Clutton had valued the Forest timber at nearly £34,000, 'all realized, except a small quantity left for ornament' by the time he entertained the Land Surveyors in July 1859. They were much pleased with what they saw: the farmsteads were conveniently designed, their sites 'judiciously selected in reference both to the occupation of the land and the beauty of the prospects'.

Some of the surveyors thought the rents somewhat high, but Mr Clutton pointed out two advantages that offset them. First, the farms were free from tithe rent charges and almost free from poor rates, because they stood in the new parish of 'Whichwood' created under the act of 1853. Secondly, as the buildings and roads were so new and well-made, it was unlikely the tenants would have to do much in the way of repairs over the next thirty-one years. There was no question but that the surveyors were impressed above all by the speed with which Wychwood was transformed. 'The extraordinary part of the scheme has been the marvellous rapidity of the execution': only sixteen months for converting nearly 2,000 acres of woodland 'effectively into farming land' and nine months later 'the first crop harvested and the first rent paid'. The report goes further into what was done on the new farms: 'The novel, skilful and economical systems adopted by some of the tenants in obtaining their first crop, especially that of Mr Belcher, has great merit, and is worthy of imitation'. The Crown Surveyor, moreover, would be only too pleased to help any landowner or surveyor 'who may desire to inspect this truly national work'.

The transformation of Wychwood did indeed attract national attention. *The Times* was moved to devote a second leader to it on 29 September 1859. This used Wychwood to debate the pros and cons of clearing the English Forests to make way for cultivable land. The main facts of the Wychwood conversion are cited again, and the conclusion offered is that such changes were good and necessary; 'The soil is made for man, and not man for the soil, and if Whichwood Forest has disappeared a British community has sprung up in its place. Men for matter is no such bad exchange'. Not all agreed, for the next day (30 September 1859) *The Times* printed a letter to the editor from 'The Ghost of Whichwood'.

The 'Ghost' resented the destruction of the Forest because he or she felt that there were thousands of less beautiful acres in England that could be reclaimed. 'My character was never called in question' – an interesting rebuttal of Arthur Young's earlier strictures – the only beings 'who wandered through my domain were a few harmless gipsies, against whom no one complained. The farmer was well pleased and satisfied with his rights of common'. A poor view was also taken of those who had supported the Act: 'My Lords Churchill and Redesdale, whom I had long fostered, deserted me in my long hour of need, and gain and greed carried the day'. The Forest had been replaced with 'turnips and Oxfordshire stone walls'.

St Michael, Leafield, by Sir
George Gilbert Scott, 1860

The physical appearance of the Forest was indeed transformed. We can still see the stone walls, the new farmsteads with royal AV crowned monograms and layouts for mixed stock and arable farming, and the 'new' or expanded settlements, as at Fordwells (with its Primitive Methodist chapel of 1864 and Norton's Terrace of 1868) and at Leafield (where a new George Gilbert Scott church of 1860 followed on the creation of the new, civil, Wychwood parish in 1858 which was included in Leafield ecclesiastical parish in 1860).

We have heard already of the demise at or before disafforestation of the communal feasts, hunts and fairs. Now there was a different leisure emphasis – hunting, and game birds, on Cornbury and other estates. This comes over particularly clearly in the diary, kept from 1875 to

1900, of John Simpson Calvertt. He took on Fairspear and High Lodge farms in 1875 on a seventeen-year lease. In 1894 he transferred Fairspear to his son John Charles and took on Langley (an ancient royal hunting lodge) where he lived until his death in 1900. His life was one of hunting three days a week, worship at Leafield Church, Tory politics, imperial enthusiasms, finely tuned deference to Lord Churchill, and working farming. Agricultural labourers feature little; Calvertt's social circle was of fellow farmers, professionals and tradesmen. His family connections were far flung. He was conscious of the Forest and its history. On 25 April 1885 he wrote of a spring day in Wychwood, 'The Blackthorn in full flower in the Forest – rode through the 'Slates Copse' cut and cleared this winter – as I ride up and down the 1,200 acres remnant of Whichwood Forest all in a piece and *no public road* whatever thro' it, I think of its History, the Hunting Ground of the Kings of England for Ages and of what sport of various kinds it afforded them, nearly all the year'.

The Forest had in some ways been opened up by its transformation. Something of this is revealed by an analysis of birthplaces of people recorded in the census returns for two Windrush valley villages by the Forest – Swinbrook (in 1851 before the enclosure of 1856) and Minster Lovell (in 1871, after enclosure). In the earlier census birthplaces are very local: outside birthplaces were concentrated in a line following the Windrush valley to Burford, Fulbrook, Witney and adjoining places, with few connections to the north where the Forest lay. By 1871 there were larger numbers of less local birthplaces, still with a strong linear, valley emphasis, but also with a noticeable northerly emphasis of places towards Chipping Norton where the Forest had lain.

General population levels remained static or increased slightly in the Wychwood villages in 1861, the first census after the transformation. Thereafter there is little to suggest that either the 'improved' farming landscape of the new Wychwood, nor the surviving elements (potting, lime burning, gloving) of the old Forest economy, were enough to

FOWLER'S FOUR-FURROW PLOUGH

buffer the Wychwood communities from general trends in rural Oxfordshire of population decline and poor agricultural returns.

To some extent this was part of a very much larger picture of agricultural depression after 1873. But it was also, as Calvertt's diary tells us, about farming an area of mixed and hungry soils and poor water supplies. Freeman argues that this was the consequence of the over-exploitation of the eighteenth-century Forest coming home to roost. When a National Nature Reserve was created in Wychwood a hundred years after the enclosure, the signs of leached soils and non-

calcareous soils were apparent. In the uncleared woodland areas of the enclosed Forest the withdrawal of deer, the end of timber growing (e.g. for ship building), and the halt to commoning produced a new ecology. Ash overtook oak, and the understorey of hawthorn grew unchecked. Elder scrub developed.

When in 1916 John Orr followed in Arthur Young's footsteps to survey the agriculture of Oxfordshire he found Wychwood a 'cold and late country of bad reputation'. A farmer told him that 'in a field of 50 acres he meets six different kinds of soil, an experience which renders cultivation difficult... he thinks it a mistake that the trees were ever grubbed up, since the return on capital expenditure has been inadequate'. East of Leafield, Orr concluded, 'is one of the least interesting parts of the country, being distinguished by few specimens of good farming and by no picturesque features... It may be unfortunate but the enclosure of Wychwood seems neither to have filled the pockets of landlords and farmers nor to have emptied Oxford gaol'.

We come full circle to Arthur Young's assertions at the start of the nineteenth century. In that time the natural ecology, the leisure pursuits, the social relations, the farming, and the landscape of Wychwood had all been radically transformed.

REFERENCES AND FURTHER READING

Belcher, C., 'Reclaiming of waste lands as instanced in Whichwood Forest', in *Journal of the Royal Agricultural Society of England*, Vol. 24, 1863, pp. 271-85.

Emery, F., *The Oxfordshire Landscape*, 1974; 'The transformation of Wychwood – some fresh evidence', in Oxfordshire Local History, Vol. 2, No. 1, 1984.

Freeman, M., 'Whichwood Forest, Oxfordshire: an episode in its recent environmental history', in *Agricultural History Review*, Vol. 45, Part II, 1997; 'Plebs or predators? Deer stealing in Whichwood Forest, Oxfordshire in the eighteenth and nineteenth centuries', in *Social History*, Vol. 21, No. 1, 1996.

Hathaway, M., 'Leisure in the English Countryside, c.1840-1914 (Unpublished research paper, 1998). I am grateful to Mark Hathaway for allowing me to refer to the work on Wychwood which forms part of his current doctoral research at Kellogg College, Oxford.

Miller, C., (ed.), *Rain and Ruin: the Diary of an Oxfordshire farmer, John Simpson Calvertt 1875–1900*, 1983.

Orr, J., *Agriculture in Oxfordshire*, 1916, pp. 51-2.

Schumer, B., *The Evolution of Wychwood to 1400*, 1984 and 1999.

Thompson, E. P., *Customs in Common*, 1991; *Whigs and Hunters: the Origins of the Block Act*, 1975.

Tiller, K., 'The Transformation of Wychwood', in Oxfordshire Local History, Vol. 1, Nos. 7 and 8 (1983 and 1984); (ed.) 'Milton and Shipton in the 19th Century', *Wychwoods History No. 3*, the Journal of the Wychwoods Local History Society, 1987.

Titterington, C. and Wilcox,T., *William Turner of Oxford (1789-1862)*, Catalogue of a touring exhibition, Oxfordshire County Museum Services, 1984, pp. 18, 34.

Young, A., *General View of the Agriculture of Oxfordshire*, 1813 edn., reprint 1969, pp. 236-9.

Wychwood Forest industries RICHARD BIDGOOD

Several industries developed in the Wychwood area which were closely related to the Forest and its raw materials. In addition to these and the more common industries such as quarrying and lime-burning, there were also unusual local industries, for example specialised steel-making and the production of Stonesfield slates.

GLOVING

Wychwood Forest became an ideal site for the production of gloves and the trade may have begun in Anglo-Saxon times. The royal manor at Woodstock and the visits of King John created the first cottage industry making riding gloves for hunting and heavy duty gloves for forest management. The needs of the gloving trade were provided by deer, sheep and pig skin, which were readily available, and by fresh water from the rivers Glyme and Windrush and from local springs and streams.

By the seventeenth century Woodstock was becoming the centre of the gloving industry in Oxfordshire, and by the eighteenth century was a major national centre of gloving. The Woodstock family of Money were among the earliest recorded glovers.

By the early nineteenth century Woodstock employed 60 to 70 men as grounders of leather and cutters of gloves, earning between 1 guinea and 30 shillings per week, and 1400 to 1500 women earning 8 to 12 shillings per week. By then production had grown rapidly from between 20 and 30 dozen pairs of gloves each week in 1800 to between 360 and 400 dozen pairs of gloves each week in total. Arthur Young wrote in 1813; 'a pair of doeskin gloves which will cost 5 shillings per pair will last a gentleman who rides daily nearly 12 months. The leather grounders have a peculiar art, in dressing the skin in such a manner as to give it at once fineness of grain and tenacity of substance'.

Woodstock was renowned for a quality product. Outworkers employed by Woodstock factories were sewing at a rate of 8 stitches to the inch and were world famous, a pair of Woodstock glovers winning an award at the Great Exhibition of 1851. By then output of gloves in Woodstock had increased to 500 dozen pairs per week. The villages of

Finstock, Stonesfield, Coombe, Long Hanborough, Ramsden and Leafield with their associated hamlets had become heavily dependent on 'outwork' to supplement income as farm wages were low and irregular. By 1890 factories were operating in Charlbury and Chipping Norton as well. By 1904 a total of 2000 women and girls, including outworkers, were employed by local gloving factories.

The main types of gloves in production in the nineteenth century were:

- Riding gloves made from heavy buckskin

- Strong driving gloves known as 'cabbies' made from tick-marked stag skin, used for example by drivers of four-in-hand stage coaches

- 'Aristocrats', gloves of high-quality soft leather 'to suit the hands of gentry'.

Business was sometimes erratic and at Woodstock the church bell was rung when a new, large contract was received as this would boost the economy of the whole town.

As late as 1920 when the firm Atherton and Clothier moved to Woodstock, local hedges could still be seen draped with sheep and goat skins bleaching in the sun. The production at this time was mainly golfing, other sports gloves and 'lammies' – sheepskin gloves with wool on the inside, a Woodstock speciality. Sadly, after a burst of production in the Second World War, production declined and the last factory closed in 1980.

WOOL

Wychwood and its environs contained large tracts of land which were used for sheep breeding and wool production. This was particularly important for Witney with its blanket trade and for Woodstock, Charlbury and surrounding villages with their gloving, breeches and belts trade.

As well as being used locally, wool was bought by middlemen and sold for export. The wealthiest of all were the Cotswold wool merchants of the fifteenth century. The Cotswold breed of sheep had a reputation for producing high quality wool. These merchants used their wealth to endow churches in the area, for example at Chipping Norton and Witney. No individually named merchants appear in Burford town records but a guild was formed which built its own chapel, now incorporated into the enlarged church. Weaving of wool was also carried out in these towns.

The huge profits available from keeping sheep encouraged a move to early enclosure of open fields, turning them to pasture. The resulting shortage of farm work created a drift of labour towards the towns. Cottages were pulled down, for example at Broadstone and Nether Chalford near Chipping Norton. Witney's blanket trade increased in the seventeenth and eighteenth centuries, and the gloving industry at Woodstock and Charlbury increased in the nineteenth century.

The main sheep breeds which proved profitable in the area in the nineteenth century were Leicester, Gloucester, Cotswold and the crossbred New Leicester. The Duke of Marlborough ran a flock of 'half Leicester, half Cotswold' crossbred sheep folded on wheat and enclosed in locally made hurdles produced from coppiced willow and hazel. He also had South Downs, a hardy breed, and Welsh which were raised for his table because of their excellent flavour.

Arthur Young, writing in 1813, records 'It may be generally estimated that every acre carries a sheep and a lamb. Perhaps on an average of the county 300 are sheared on a farm of 400 acres'. His comments were made in passing, and may not have applied to areas where large amounts of woodland still remained.

CHARCOAL

Charcoal is the black carbonised residue of partially burned wood produced under conditions that prevent it bursting into flame. The main uses of charcoal were as a fuel in smelting and as a constituent in the production of gunpowder.

Charcoal burning has been a skilled craft for well over 1000 years and the characteristic domed kilns of charcoal burners were until comparatively recently a common sight in many woodland areas including Wychwood. The kilns, from 2–7 metres (7–24 ft) in diameter, were formed from layers of thin coppice wood placed around a central stake. Hazel, sycamore, hornbeam, ash and oak were all used, but alder was considered the best material. These layers were heavily covered by turf. The kiln was ignited, sometimes by hot coal or charcoals, and the draught was carefully controlled through gaps in the turf. To ensure there was no flame, water was poured into the kiln to produce steam which doused any flames and drove air from the kiln. When properly alight the kiln was sealed with more damp turf.

Charcoal kilns would smoulder for days while moisture was removed from the wood and combustible gases were extracted through a vent at the top of the dome. The charcoal burner lived, often in a primitive hut, by his hearth which he tended night and day until the process was complete. Then the turfs would be removed, allowing the iridescent charcoal to cool ready for packing.

When used as a fuel charcoal glows red-hot and burns with very little flame. In a forge or furnace it can become white-hot as the heat intensifies. Its commercial importance in medieval and Tudor times equalled that of coal in the Industrial Revolution, and manufacturing centres developed in areas such as the Forest of Dean in Gloucestershire and the Weald in Kent. Locally it is believed that the Woodstock steel industry used Wychwood charcoal as a fuel.

POTTERY

The existence of clay in various parts of the Wychwood area led to the development of a pottery industry which is believed to be pre-Roman in origin. Thirty kiln sites in all had been identified in the Oxford region by 1974. Fragments of both red and black pottery lie near the barrow at Slate Pits Copse, in the remnant of Wychwood Forest. These are hand-made, not wheel-made, and may be the remains of vessels used to hold food at burial ceremonies.

In the medieval period the Jurassic clay which occurs in isolated patches at Leafield and Bladon began to be exploited for pottery making. The clay was dug from pits by hand. There is no Oxfordshire evidence of machine digging. A clay spade, made of wood or iron with its centre removed to reduce sticking, was used to pare slices of clay from the walls of the pit. The clay was dug in winter and stored in the open, where it was regularly turned over by hand to allow wind and frost action to work upon it.

To bring it to a dough-like consistency the clay was wetted and mixed using a pug mill, a piece of machinery somewhat resembling an old-fashioned cast iron kitchen mincer, driven by a series of cogs. At

Leafield the pug mill was powered by a horse. Wetted clay fed into the top of a rotating drum was sliced and mixed by revolving knives and forced out at the bottom as a smooth dough. If required, a blend of clays could be made at this stage.

Pots were constructed by hand on a wheel. 'Cutter Franklin' made pots and pans on a wheel just beyond the Baptist Chapel on Shipton Road, Leafield, in the early twentieth century. There was another pottery opposite, nowadays called Chimney End. Kilns for firing the pottery used charcoal from the Forest as fuel. The pottery produced was plain dusky red-brown utility ware, used locally and also transported for sale around Oxfordshire and parts of Buckinghamshire. Hawkers travelled the neighbourhoods, selling 'Field Town Cha'ney', domestic pottery for cooking use. Bricks may also have been made locally.

STEEL

Steel making is a surprising industry recorded in the Wychwood area. Nothing remains of the buildings where it was made in Woodstock during the eighteenth and early nineteenth centuries. Arthur Young records in 1813 that a Mr Metcalf introduced the manufacture of polished steel in the mid-eighteenth century, although its origins may have been earlier. Certainly it was a flourishing industry for a time, employing many hands, but it suffered severely from the cheapness with which similar articles, namely scissors, watch chains and trinkets, could be produced by machinery in Birmingham and Sheffield. Woodstock concentrated on elegant hand-made items for the discerning customer, but by 1813 only ten people were employed, earning no more than 1 to $1\frac{1}{2}$ guineas a week.

Woodstock polished steel was made from old horseshoe nails which were formed into small bars and worked up into the various objects being produced. Its lustre was extreme and it could be re-polished to its original brilliance at a trifling expense even when covered with rust. A Woodstock steel chain weighing only two ounces sold for £170 in about 1810. A box in which the freedom of the borough was presented to Lord Viscount Cliefden at the beginning of the nineteenth century cost 30 guineas and a garter star for His Grace the Duke of Marlborough cost 50 guineas. 'The number and fineness of the studs, each screwed by hand, enhanced the value and the expense of Woodstock polished steel articles', says Young. 'Even pairs of scissors sold at 5 shillings to 3 guineas'. He confirmed that despite its desirability, the manufacturer could not maintain a profitable business against mass production.

Some surviving articles can be seen in the Oxfordshire County Museum at Woodstock.

STONESFIELD SLATES

Some beds of the Great Oolite limestone of the Cotswolds produce excellent building stone, and others provide thin layers of rock which can be split upon exposure to frost, thus providing stone roofing tiles. Locally these were produced at Stonesfield, where level galleries and subsequently mines were dug to reach these bands of stone. The term slate is actually a misnomer, since the stone is not a slate in the geological sense – 'tilestone' would more accurate. Tiles of a range of sizes were produced, from small ones used near the ridge to massive tiles at the bottom of the roof.

Stonesfield slates are believed to have been used in the construction of Roman buildings such as the villa at Ditchley. The discovery of the process of splitting the stones by frost action is likely to have occurred in the late sixteenth century. The earliest written reference, by Dr Robert Plot, in 1677 suggests that the industry was already well-developed by then. Of the stone, he says it is 'dug first in thick cakes, about Michaelmas time, or before, to be [exposed] all the winter and receive the frosts which makes it cleave in the spring following into thinner plates'.

In 1705 Stonesfield Manor was granted along with other estates to the Duke of Marlborough who since that time has held the mineral rights, which include the 'right to search' and 'rights to work' from time to time.

By the early nineteenth century, 10% of the population of Stonesfield was engaged in the slate industry. Research by Bagley (1965) showed that 139 men over the age of twenty from the village were working in the industry in 1831, of whom 20 were full-time slate makers. However, by the early twentieth century the industry had declined as a result from competition from other materials, and Spratt's Barn Pit to the west of the village finally closed in 1911.

It is worth recording that a side industry had developed in the extraction and sale of fossils. In 1860 Marshall describes Stonesfield village as a succession of fossil shops. High quality fossils were sold to visitors from Oxford University, and those of lesser quality were cleaned and sold to tourists.

REFERENCES AND ACKNOWLEDGEMENTS

Aston, M., B.A., *Stonesfield Slate*, 1974.
Gretton, Mary Sturge, *Burford Past and Present*, 1945.
Young, Arthur, *General View of Agriculture of Oxford*, 1813.

4 Some Wychwood legends, stories and folklore

CHRISTINE BLOXHAM

This tomb doth here enclose
The world's most beauteous rose,
Rose passing sweet erewhile,
Now naught but odour vile.

This is the epitaph of one of the most famous royal mistresses, Rosamund Clifford, who is said to have lived for many years in hiding at Woodstock Palace and been buried at Godstow nunnery on the outskirts of Oxford. Her story is so intertwined with legend that the truth will never be known, but there are a few historical clues which give gleams of insight.

Henry II so enjoyed the park at Woodstock that he enlarged the hunting lodge into a full-scale royal palace, and set up the 'new' town to provide accommodation and services for his courtiers. As well as the main palace buildings, he created a bower, fashionable as a haven from the formality of court life, based around the spring at Everswell. It probably included a group of rooms and a cloister, all surrounded by high walls. Later, orchards and a herb garden were added, giving rise to the legend of a 'maze' in which Rosamund was hidden.

According to this legend Rosamund was secretly married to Henry, not knowing that he was king, and when he later married the newly divorced Eleanor for her dowry, he hid Rosamund away. It is more likely that she was merely his favourite mistress, hidden away for his pleasure. Legend says that in 1176 Henry was in a hurry one day as he left the bower and a skein of Rosamund's embroidery silk caught his spur, leaving a trail into the centre of the maze. Eleanor, wandering past the entrance, noticed the thread and carefully made her plans. She drugged a guarding knight, followed the silk, and pounced on the shocked and terrified Rosamund, offering her the stark choice between taking poison or retiring to the nunnery at Godstow. Some versions say Rosamund chose the poison, with her body being buried at Godstow. The king had left the palace before Rosamund was discovered, and on his return he was devastated to hear of her death. He went straight to Godstow, where he demanded that her grave be opened to say farewell to his beloved. Soon he regretted this rash act, because when the coffin was opened a large toad was discovered sitting between her breasts and an adder was coiled around her waist. The stench was appalling – hence the last line of Rosamund's epitaph.

However much of this must be legend, as it is now thought that Eleanor and Rosamund never actually met!

◆ ◆ ◆ ◆ ◆

As well as Fair Rosamund's Well, another reputedly sacred well is Ladywell, south of Wilcote. An avenue of ancient pollarded ash trees leads to the well, which local people traditionally visited on Palm Sunday to make liquorice water.

Tradition links several villages with wells in Wychwood. Leafield villagers used to go to a well in the Forest on Easter Monday to make 'Spanish Water', and people from Charlbury did so on Palm Sunday. Spanish liquorice was mixed with sugar, peppermint and boiling water to make a cure-all, which was often decanted into small bottles of 'spring medicine' especially for the children.

THE ASH AVENUE
LEADING TO LADYWELL

◆ ◆ ◆ ◆ ◆

Whitsun was another particularly significant time in Wychwood. Local villagers had a ancient right to hunt once a year and this was done, under careful supervision of the keepers, on Whit Monday. At midnight on Whit Sunday the villagers began to blow 'peeling horns', each carefully constructed from a coil of soaked green willow bark, peeled spirally and held together with thorns, with a bassoon reed inserted in the narrow end. Some of these horns still survive in the Pitt Rivers Museum. Early on Whit Monday men from the neighbouring villages set off to hunt deer. The first man in at the kill was allowed to keep the antlers. Three deer were killed in all, the first going to Hailey, the second to Crawley and the third to Witney. After the beasts had been skinned all the participants scrambled for a piece of the skin, which was supposed to bring the owner good luck, and displayed them on their hats.

LADYWELL, A SACRED
WELL SOUTH OF
WILCOTE

After the hunt, proceedings adjourned to Ducklington where festivities – including dancing, morris dancing, fights between local champions and

races – continued for several days. The venison was cooked and eaten on the following Saturday.

❖ ❖ ❖ ❖ ❖

Morris dancing continued to be a popular recreation locally, the dancers being agricultural labourers and craftsmen. There were several teams, mostly consisting of six men, in the Wychwood area, many of whom continued to dance until at least the 1870s. The sword bearer of the Leafield team, like the Bampton sword bearer today, carried a cake and people paid for slices which they ate with their penknife. This tradition seems to have been tied up with fertility, and even today women who want a baby are encouraged to secure a slice of Bampton Morris men's cake. There were also teams at Field Assarts, Finstock, Shipton- and Ascott-under-Wychwood, Ducklington, Brize Norton and Spelsbury who danced around the Wychwood villages at Whitsun. Morris dancing has revived and Charlbury still has a team.

❖ ❖ ❖ ❖ ❖

Wychwood has its share of ghosts, and Cornbury Park is said to be haunted by the ghost of Amy Robsart. Amy was the wife of Robert Dudley, Queen Elizabeth's favourite. She was kept out of the way whilst her husband and the queen dallied at leisure. The royal flirtation became notorious, and those that were jealous of Dudley began a rumour that he intended to kill his wife. Whilst staying at Cumnor Place on the 8th of September 1560, after releasing her servants to enjoy themselves at nearby Abingdon Fair, Amy was found by the returning servants lying at the foot of three flights of stairs, with a broken neck.

Amy's ghost not only haunted Cumnor, but made a spectacular appearance – perhaps wreaking vengeance for her mistreatment in life by Robert Dudley – at Cornbury where he was staying in 1588. Her ghost appeared to him as he was hunting in Wychwood Forest, warning him that he would join her in death within ten days. He duly died shortly afterwards. Amy is said to have haunted Cornbury ever since, and a sighting of her is a warning of sudden death.

❖ ❖ ❖ ❖ ❖

Legends of ghostly dogs, often in which human souls have taken refuge, abound in Oxfordshire. Fairspear House near Leafield was said to be so haunted – the maids of the house feared to wait for their young men by the side gate because of the great black dog which prowled the lane. It also appeared in Leafield churchyard, where it was seen many times leaping over the wall and running off northwards. Leafield had been at the heart of Wychwood, so possibly the legend of the dog was a cautionary tale to deter children from wandering into the Forest woodland, or perhaps it was the ghost of an ancient mastiff used for hunting in the Forest. At North Leigh a similar black dog has been seen in quite recent times.

Often it was thought that these dogs personified the souls of dead humans, and could be 'laid' in the same way as more ordinary ghosts; otherwise they were described as the Devil himself.

◆ ◆ ◆ ◆ ◆

Another type of ghost, the spectral coach, has appeared in Wychwood. These visions may carry on the tradition of the Wild Hunt, feared throughout Europe since pagan times, when Woden hunted the countryside bringing disaster in his wake.

In the seventeenth century, Lord and Lady Tanfield were unscrupulous and rapacious inhabitants of Burford. He was a judge, yet when he acquired Great Tew he unfairly deprived the inhabitants of many rights which they had held since time immemorial, impoverishing them. He is also said to have stolen the 'Poors' Plot' at Wilcote, but here he got a taste of his own medicine – the ghosts of the Lord and Lady who originally gave the plot to the poor chased him in their ghostly chariot, crying 'cast up! cast up!' in an attempt to persuade him to repent and return the plot to the poor. Whether or not the judge did so is not recorded. As he and his wife were so universally unpopular, it is not surprising that their ghosts haunt several places. At North Leigh they have been seen driving a ghostly coach and four. They also haunted the people of Burford, who were so terrified by the apparition that they had the ghost exorcised. Seven clergymen, armed with bell, book and candle, trapped the spirits inside a bottle which they flung under the first arch of Burford bridge. According to legend, if the river bed under the arch ever becomes dry the spirits will be released.

◆ ◆ ◆ ◆ ◆

A dire fate also awaited the Dunsden brothers, Tom, Dick and Harry, who were born of yeoman stock at the old Manor House, Fulbrook near Burford in the mid-eighteenth century. They became highwaymen, apparently after they themselves suffered injustice, possibly over land rights. They started their life of crime in a small way, robbing local farmers and hiding their booty in Wychwood Forest as well as in a cave near Icomb. They grew more ambitious and robbed the Oxford coach of £500. However, they also grew careless and their plans to rob Tangley

Hall became known. Forewarned, the inhabitants arranged for several constables to hide in the house. Unaware, the Dunsdens crept up to the house and Dick quietly slid back the shutter in the front door and thrust his arm in to try and open the door. To his horror his arm was firmly grabbed from the inside, and after a struggle the only way for him to procure his release was to cut it off. No more is heard of him, and he must have died of his wounds.

The remaining Dunsdens appear to have been tolerated by local people. One story tells that when their shoes needed mending, they took them to Fifield at the dead of night and left them on the cobbler's doorstep, collecting the finished shoes the next night and leaving a generous fee.

However, their bold behaviour was their downfall. On Whit Sunday 1784 they went drinking and gambling with the local people at Capps Lodge near Burford and when a quarrel arose they found the rest of the party against them. The local ostler, William Harding, attempted to defuse the situation but the Dunsdens fired their pistols and tried to escape. A constable arrived and they were captured and sent for trial at Gloucester Assize where they were hanged. To deter others from following their evil ways their bodies were subsequently gibbetted on a tree near Capps Lodge and for weeks afterwards the favourite Sunday occupation of the locals was to see how much remained of the bodies.

◆ ◆ ◆ ◆ ◆

A happier event was the mock mayormaking in Old Woodstock, on the Chipping Norton side of the River Glyme. Rosamund's Henry II had created the medieval new town of Woodstock on the other bank, for his courtiers and attendants. New Woodstock grew and acquired borough status in the fifteenth century. Those who lived in the old town were disenfranchised from electing the town mayor, and retaliated by electing their own 'mock mayor' in comic opposition to his legal counterpart. To show their contempt for the genuine civic authority, the mock mayor was often a drunken reprobate. He was traditionally elected on the local feast day, the Monday following the first Sunday after the 19th of September. The tradition continued, and by 1896 the celebrations began with a cricket match and sports followed by lunch at the Rose and Crown. Then came the election, and during the evening the mock mayor was chaired down Old Woodstock hill, round 'New Woodstock', where he naturally visited all the pubs, before being ingloriously tipped into the River Glyme.

Christine Bloxham's book *Mayday to Mummers – Oxfordshire Seasonal Customs* is published by the Wychwood Press in Autumn 2000.

ALAN SPICER

GEOLOGY AND LANDFORM

The eleventh-century Norman royal Forest covered approximately one hundred square miles or 30,000 hectares (about 60,000 acres), a large portion of today's West Oxfordshire. It was bounded by the rivers Glyme, Thames, Windrush and the Sars Brook. The north of this region consists of a plateau of Great Oolitic Limestone, laid down in the Jurassic geological period between 195 and 136 million years ago. This plateau which is on the eastern edge of the Cotswold dip slope is, within the area of the Norman Forest, at its highest near Chipping Norton where it reaches 250 metres (700 feet). It descends to about 150 metres (nearly 500 feet) towards the flat riverside meadows of the Thames Valley. Dissected by the river valleys of the Windrush, Evenlode and Glyme, the limestone upland is eroded to reveal the bluish lias clay deposited in deeper water during the Jurassic period. The limestone is rich in marine fossils of shell fish and even dinosaur remains.

The harder layers of this limestone, quarried for example at Taynton and in the past at Barrington, are amongst the best building stones in England, and have been much used in Oxford as well as at local large mansions including Blenheim Palace and Cornbury Park. Another product of the Great Oolite, Stonesfield slate, provides the traditional roofing material for the area. At the top of the Great Oolite series, the Forest Marble formation, quarried near Bladon, has provided much of the stone for construction in Oxford since the Second World War. Cornbrash and other sandier seams of limestone have provided materials for drystone and rubble walling.

Much of this Cotswold plateau is now intensively farmed, with arable crops or improved grassland flourishing on the surface above the rubbly oolitic and cornbrash limestones.

The junction of the porous limestone with the impervious lias clay below results in the emergence of numerous springs which form streams flowing into the rivers of the area. A younger layer of Oxford clay covers the limestone in the south east of the region, and extensive gravel and alluvial deposits mark the former courses of the rivers

THE WOODLANDS AT
CORNBURY, SEEN FROM
NEAR CHARLBURY

Windrush and Thames. These deposits have been exploited in recent times for gravel and sand extraction, creating new wetland habitats when worked out.

WOODLANDS

Most of the larger areas of woodland nowadays within the Wychwood area are part of large estates, including Cornbury, Blenheim, Ditchley, Kiddington, Bruern and Heythrop. About half is ancient woodland – that is, on a site which has been continuously wooded for at least 400 years. During the twentieth century about one third of this has been felled, and replanted with conifers for commercial forestry. Other woodlands of both conifers and broadleaves have been planted since the nineteenth-century disafforestation, mostly for timber and game coverts.

In addition there are are a number of small woodlands. Some of these are ancient and, like their larger counterparts, are remnants of the medieval or even Norman Wychwood. Unfortunately their small size and isolation renders them less likely to sustain healthy populations of animals, birds and flowers. This is also true of some of the larger woodlands which have often become separated from their neighbours by large tracts of arable farmland.

The Wychwood ancient woodlands were traditionally managed as

74

coppice, latterly at least as coppice with standards. Hazel, ash and field maple were the usual coppice trees. Individual copses were cut down to ground level in cycles, which could be up to twenty-five years in duration. This provided a supply of fuel, fencing material, poles for wood products and thatching spars. Oaks were left to grow on as standards to be used as building timber. Sometimes pure coppice was practised, mostly hazel, which was usually worked on a six- to twelve-year cycle. Coppicing allows light to reach the woodland floor and stimulates a profusion of spring flowers to germinate from dormant seeds. This floral display continues for about five years until the regrowth of the coppiced trees shades out the plants.

The increasing availability of coal and other alternative fossil fuels in the twentieth century has led to an almost complete cessation of coppicing. However, it is being revived at Foxholes nature reserve at Bruern and at Holly Grove near Wilcote.

The woodlands typically have a wide range of smaller trees and shrubs as an understorey beneath the dominant oak and ash. Dogwood, spindleberry, holly, wayfaring tree, hawthorn and blackthorn are often present; the wild service tree, a member of the sorbus family whose broad leaves have sharply cut triangular lobes, is generally uncommon in Oxfordshire but occurs in modest numbers in some of the older woodlands in the Wychwood area.

In addition to the plants traditionally found in these Cotswold woods such as bluebell, dog's mercury, yellow archangel, wood anemone and primrose, the ancient woodlands are refuges for a number of scarce and striking plants including green hellebore, herb THE WILD SERVICE TREE

paris, toothwort, meadow saffron, greater butterfly orchid and early purple orchid. Many of these have poor powers of dispersal and are restricted to the ancient woodlands.

Birds such as nuthatch, woodpeckers and tree creepers favour woodlands with old or dead trees where nest holes and copious supplies of invertebrates as food are available. Woodcock and buzzards breed in the larger wooded areas. The distinctive call of the chiff-chaff is heard

WOODPECKER

in early spring and these woodlands are home to many small birds including tits, warblers and wrens.

Several types of deer can be regularly seen in the area. Most common are fallow and the diminutive muntjac, with smaller numbers of roe. There is a large herd of fallow deer at Cornbury Park, with a few sika deer. Badgers and foxes are found throughout the region. The dormouse is now probably very scarce, due to the decline in hazel coppicing. Two rare snails, the bulin and the much larger 'Roman' snail, are occasionally to be found in the older woodlands.

Uncommon species of butterfly, such as the white admiral and wood white, occur in the Foxholes nature reserve at Bruern.

The historic parks within the Forest area contain fine specimens of aged oaks and other trees, which are colonised by many species of rare lichens and invertebrates, particularly beetles. Blenheim has an area of wood pasture with many veteran oaks set in grassland and bracken, a habitat reminiscent of the heyday of the royal Forest.

Riverside woodlands often include alders, which attract siskins to feed on their catkins. Some of the woodland clothing the steep hillsides of the lower Evenlode valley contain a rich spring flora including the rare yellow star of Bethlehem, a member of the lily family.

Coniferous woodlands, planted to provide softwood timber, attract coal-tits, siskins, goldcrests and sometimes redpolls. The winter shelter provided by these mostly evergreen woods may aid the survival of many birds, including owls – which are sadly reducing in numbers as their habitats decline.

Scrub, dominated by hawthorn and blackthorn, is not extensive in the Wychwood area. Chiefly it is found in disused quarries, gravel pits and along the borders of railway lines. It is valuable for a number of birds including whitethroat, blackcap, garden and willow warblers and the occasional grasshopper warbler. Gorse scrub survives on the acid gravelly soil of North Leigh Common.

HEDGEROWS

Many of the hedges in the area are composed of a wide variety of trees and shrubs, typical of ancient woodland. These include field maple, midland hawthorn, holly, crab apple, wych elm and wild service. Such hedges are often associated with a number of woodland plants that indicate their origin as remnants of former woodlands which were cleared to provide settlements or farmland. Studies have shown that locally wood anemone, yellow archangel, goldilocks buttercup and wood spurge can be linked to locations of former Wychwood woodlands. Indeed, remnant hedges may confirm evidence

from maps and documents about the location of former woodlands. A
network of such woodland relic hedgerows can be seen between
Charlbury and Stonesfield.

WOOD PASTURE AT
BLENHEIM

Hedges with a dense continuous structure provide a wildlife habitat
resembling that of the woodland edge. The traditional management of
hedgerows by laying has declined greatly in recent decades, but is
currently being reintroduced in order to thicken up the structure of tall
straggly hedges. These layed hedges are more beneficial to wildlife than
their straggly predecessors, and will attract a variety of birds, mammals
and insects which benefit from the fruit and seed stores, nest sites and
the provision of shelter in these thicker hedges. Hedges containing
mature trees are particularly valuable for nesting kestrels, woodpeckers
and little owls. Moth caterpillars feeding on particular hedge shrubs
and plants are a vital food source for newly hatched tits,
yellowhammers and whitethroats. Hedges situated on grassy banks,
beside ditches or streams and those bordering verges and green lanes
provide refuge and a corridor for safe migration through the
countryside.

LIMESTONE GRASSLAND

Limestone grassland was previously more extensive in the form of downland covering the higher ground between the river valleys, but is now restricted to small fragments chiefly on steep riverside banks, road verges, green lanes, disused quarries, railway embankments and within some historic parks. These typical Cotswold grasslands, 'unimproved' with fertilisers and pesticides, produce a delightful display of summer flowers attracting butterflies, moths and other nectar-seeking insects. Frequently knapweeds, field scabious, thyme, dwarf thistle, quaking grass, cowslip and rock rose will be found; different mixes of these and other lime-tolerant plants occur at different sites throughout Wychwood. Other less common plants occur at particular sites: these include pyramidal and bee orchids, harebell, kidney and horseshoe vetches, wild liquorice and autumn gentian. Two rare and protected plants are found at various locations within the Wychwood region: meadow clary, a spectacular blue salvia, has its stronghold in this area; and downy woundwort is restricted to this part of England.

These grasslands support a variety of attractive butterflies and moths, their caterpillars feeding on specific flowers and grasses. Common blue, marbled white, large skipper, small heath and meadow brown butterflies and the red-spotted burnet moth occur in large numbers at some of these sites.

LIMESTONE GRASSLAND AT STONESFIELD COMMON

A number of limestone grassland areas have been designated as

nature reserves, and several sections of roadside verges in the region with uncommon flowers have been marked with posts as linear nature reserves by Oxfordshire County Council. Many of the roadside verges throughout the Forest area reveal in June and July a fine array of the sky-blue meadow cranesbill, a wild geranium.

A handsome display of limestone flowers and insects may be seen throughout the summer at Stonesfield Common, a Site of Special Scientific Interest (SSSI).

NEUTRAL GRASSLAND

The clay and alluvial soils of the river valleys of the Glyme, Evenlode and Windrush contain some hay meadows and wet pastures of unimproved grassland. These damp meadows attract wading birds such as snipe, lapwing and redshank to feed on snails, worms and other invertebrates, by probing their bills in the soft mud of the fields. The

A COUNTY NATURE RESERVE ON A ROAD-SIDE VERGE

shy curlew is at present unfortunately only found resident in the Upper Thames Valley to the south of Wychwood.

Typical flowering plants for these neutral grasslands are great burnet, devil's bit scabious, cuckoo flower, common spotted orchid and lady's mantle. The tiny adder's tongue fern is a rarer member of this flora. The spectacular snake's head fritillary, formerly widespread in the river valleys of the Thames and its tributaries, is now only present at Ducklington on the edge of the Norman Forest.

Throughout this part of West Oxfordshire there are many small areas of rough, unmanaged grassland, either calcareous or neutral, on road verges, green lanes, railway embankments and disused quarries. Dominated by grasses such as false oat and cocksfoot with tall stems of hogweed and cow parsley, they harbour voles, mice and shrews, and a variety of snails, slugs, spiders and beetles which attract owls, kestrels and foxes. Skylarks may breed here and seed heads and insects provide food for migrating and overwintering birds of many kinds. Rare plants such as the Cotswold pennycress and the dark blue wild grape hyacinth have been discovered on such sites.

HEATHLAND

Although no true heath remains in West Oxfordshire, there are a number of places where areas of bracken, gorse scrub and acid grassland still exist. These remnants of former heathland are typified by the presence of sheep's sorrel, heath bedstraw, tormentil and other acid-tolerant plants.

Some of these areas still retain the name Heath, for example Bladon Heath and Finstock Heath.

Small patches of common heather or ling have been discovered on some sites and opportunities may arise to reinstate some of this heathland. Due to its paucity locally, this habitat supports invertebrates which are vary rare in the region. North Leigh Common, a remnant of the once extensive Eynsham Heath, is owned by West Oxfordshire District Council, which is restoring it.

RIVERS AND WETLANDS

The River Thames and its tributaries the Windrush, Evenlode and Glyme comprise a large part of the Upper Thames Tributaries Environmentally Sensitive Area (ESA). This designation recognises the wildlife and landscape importance of this river system. In addition a number of streams including the Coldwell, Coombe, Taston and Sars Brook arise from springs at the junction of the limestone and the impervious clay in the region's river valleys. Floating water crowfoot,

emergent yellow flag (iris), arrowhead and water plantain, together with bankside purple loosestrife, meadowsweet and hemp agrimony produce a colourful display of summer flowers.

ALDERS ON THE RIVER EVENLODE

Alders and crack willows, with their purple and orange twigs in winter, are characteristic riverside trees providing seeds, nesting and roosting habitats for small birds and sometimes mallards. Colourful dragon and damselflies hunt along rivers seeking their prey in the form of smaller insects, especially flies. Caddis and mayflies emerge from the rivers in late spring and are taken by trout. A range of other fish, including pike, tench, roach, rudd and perch, also inhabit these rivers, thriving on aquatic invertebrates.

KINGFISHER

Kingfishers are occasionally seen diving for minnows and other small fish, which indicates the relatively unpolluted nature of these waters. Mute swans, mallards, herons, coots and moorhens are often encountered.

The large rosy-pink heads of the flowering rush are found at a few locations. The native white clawed crayfish, water vole and dipper are now sadly very scarce, whilst an otter may occasionally pass through. In the future it is hoped that otters may breed in artificial holts which have been constructed in remote, protected parts of these river valleys.

Expanses of open water are distributed throughout the region. Eight historic parks each contain at least one lake. Blenheim, the largest, was created from the dammed River Glyme. In addition to the more common river birds, these lakes are frequented by great crested grebes and visiting teal, widgeon, shoveller and gadwall ducks as well as the occasional cormorant. Large numbers of Canada geese breed on some of these lakes, which also attract passing rarities. The surrounds of the lake provide habitat essential for frog, toad, common newt and grass snake. Floating and lakeside vegetation include, in addition to the more common riverside plants, mare's tail, bulrush, water forget-me-not and bur-reed. Farm ponds provide smaller scale but similar conditions for wildlife. Gravel extractions from the lower Windrush valley between Witney and the Thames is creating water-filled pits, often with considerable marginal damp and scrub habitats. These are becoming increasingly important areas for a wide range of aquatic and terrestrial flora and fauna, particularly where there is minimal human disturbance.

Marshland is uncommon since much of the region is covered by free-draining limestone and many former wet areas in the river valleys have been systematically drained in modern times. Where waterlogged ground still persists adjacent to springlines and streams some

distinctive wildlife may be found. Pink-flowered ragged robin, yellow marsh marigold, watermint, marsh bedstraw and occasionally southern marsh orchids are restricted to such vulnerable and isolated habitats. Wading birds, including snipe, redshank and lapwing, occur and may still breed in a few places.

THE LAKE AT BLENHEIM

Where tall vegetation has survived along banks and edges of lakes and ponds, beds of the common reed, great pond sedge, reed canary and sweet grass provide nesting and shelter for reed and sedge warblers and occasional reed buntings. Woodstock Town Meadows are a good place to see some of this wetland wildlife. The wildlife of the River Evenlode can be appreciated on foot by following the Oxfordshire Way between Charlbury and Ascott-under-Wychwood and, on foot also, from Finstock to Combe. The Windrush is best viewed between Minster Lovell and Ducklington just south of Witney. The Thames path from Newbridge to Eynsham follows a fine section of the Thames.

TOWNS AND VILLAGES

Settlements in the Wychwood area support a wide variety of wildlife which is often absent from the large areas of intensively managed surrounding farmland. House martins, swallows, swifts and bats all nest and roost in suitable dwellings. The Cotswold stone walls and farm

FERNS ON A
DRY-STONE WALL

MARSH MARIGOLD

buildings provide micro-habitats for plants such as the rustyback fern, wall-rue spleenwort and ivy-leaved toadflax. Churchyards and cemeteries often contain areas of unimproved grassland and their walls and tombstones are colonised by a variety of lichens and mosses. Gardens can provide a huge variety of micro-habitats from log piles to ponds, compost heaps to shrubberies. Many of the local communities now have nature reserves or wildlife conservation areas with either a single or more often a mixture of habitats. Examples can be found at Charlbury in the Wigwell Valley, Woodstock and Witney Town Meadows.

DISUSED QUARRIES

The former quarries at Stanton Harcourt, Charlbury, Long Hanborough and Stonesfield are designated as Geological SSSIs due to the rock formations and fossils that they contain. They also provide refuges for a variety of the region's wildlife.

84

ARABLE FARMLAND

Uncultivated field margins still support examples of now generally rare cornfield weeds which include blue pimpernel, red hemp nettle and round-leaved fluellen. Brown hares and badgers dwell on this land, and barn owls, song thrushes, turtle doves, linnets, lapwings and skylarks are still to be seen – but usually in much lower numbers even than in recent decades.

FURTHER READING

Dunn, A. J., *The Flora of Ditchley – Wild Flowers of an Oxfordshire Estate*, 1993. Information on availability from the author.

Hawker, G., *An Ecological Audit of West Oxfordshire*, 1998, West Oxfordshire District Council.

Action for Wildlife – Oxfordshire's Biodiversity Action Plan, 1998, Oxfordshire Nature Conservation Forum.

VIEW OF WYCHWOOD FOREST AT LANKERIDGE FROM VERNON J. WATNEY's *Cornbury and the Forest of Wychwood*, 1910

One hundred flowering plants of the Wychwood area

LATIN NAME	ENGLISH NAME
Adoxa moschatellina	Moschatel
Agrimonia eupatoria	Agrimony
Ajuga reptans	Self-heal
Alchemilla vulgaris	Lady's mantle
Alisma plantago-aquatica	Water plantain
Alliaria petiolata	Garlic mustard
Allium ursinum	Ramsons
Anacamptis pyramidalis	Pyramidal orchid
Anemone nemoralis	Wood anemone
Angelica sylvestris	Wild angelica
Anthyllius vulneraria	Kidney vetch
Apium nodiflorum	Fool's watercress
Arum maculatum	Lords and ladies
Astragalus glycyphyllos	Wild liquorice
Atropa belladona	Deadly nightshade
Betonica officinalis	Betony
Bryonia dioica	White bryony
Caltha palustris	Marsh marigold
Campanula glomerata	Clustered bellflower
Campanula rotundifolia	Harebell
Cardamine pratensis	Cuckoo flower
Centaurea nigra	Black knapweed
Centaurea scabiosa	Greater knapweed
Chrysanthemum leucanthemum	Ox-eye daisy
Cirsium eriophorum	Woolly thistle
Cirsium palustre	Marsh thistle
Clinopodium vulgare	Wild basil
Colchicum autumnale	Meadow saffron
Conipodium majus	Pignut
Conium maculatum	Hemlock
Cymbalaria muralis	Ivy-leaved toadflax
Dactylorhiza fuchsii	Common spotted orchid
Dactylorhiza praetermissa	Southern marsh orchid
Daucus carota	Wild carrot
Dipsacus fullonum	Teasel
Echium vulgare	Viper's bugloss
Eupatorium cinnabinum	Hemp agrimony
Endymion non-scriptus	Bluebell
Euphorbia amygdaloides	Wood spurge
Filipendula ulmaria	Meadowsweet
Gagea lutea	Yellow star of Bethlehem
Galeobdolon lutea	Yellow archangel
Galium odoratum	Woodruff
Galium palustre	Marsh bedstraw
Galium saxatile	Heath bedstraw
Galium verum	Lady's bedstraw
Gentianella amarella	Autumn gentian
Geranium pratense	Meadow cranesbill

Geum urbanum	Wood avens
Helianthemum chamaecistus	Rock rose
Helleborus viridis	Green hellebore
Hippocrepis comosa	Horseshoe vetch
Hippuris vulgaris	Mare's tail
Hypericum perforatum	Perforate St John's wort
Iris pseudacorus	Yellow iris
Knautia arvensis	Field scabious
Lathrea squamaria	Toothwort
Lathyrus pratensis	Meadow vetchling
Linaria vulgaris	Common toadflax
Linum catharticum	Fairy flax
Lotus corniculatus	Bird's-foot trefoil
Lychnis flos-cuculi	Ragged robin
Lythrum salicaria	Purple loosestrife
Medicago lupulina	Black medick
Mentha aquatica	Water mint
Mercuralis perennis	Dog's mercury
Muscari atlanticum	Grape hyacinth
Myosotis scorpioides	Water forget-me-not
Odonites verna	Red bartsia
Onobrychis viciifolia	Sainfoin
Ononis repens	Rest harrow
Ophrys apifera	Bee orchid
Orchis maculata	Early purple orchid
Origanum vulgare	Marjoram
Paris quadrifolia	Herb paris
Pimpinella saxifraga	Burnet saxifrage
Plantethera chlorantha	Greater butterfly orchid
Polygala vulgaris	Common milkwort
Potentilla erecta	Tormentil
Poterium sanguisorba	Salad burnet
Primula veris	Cowslip
Primula vulgaris	Primrose
Pulicaria dysenterica	Common fleabane
Ranunculus auricomus	Goldilocks buttercup
R. fluitans	Water crowfoot
Reseda lutea	Wild mignonette
Rhinanthus minor	Yellow rattle
Rumex acetosella	Sheep's sorrel
Sagittaria sagittifolia	Arrowhead
Salvia pratensis	Meadow clary
Scabiosa columbaria	Small scabious
Sisymbrium officinale	Hedge mustard
Stachys germanica	Downy woundwort
Stachys sylvatica	Hedge woundwort
Succisa pratensis	Devil's bit scabious
Symphytum officinale	Common comfrey
Thymus drucei	Wild thyme
Veronica beccabunga	Brooklime
Veronica chamaedrys	Germander speedwell
Vicia sepium	Bush vetch

6 Wychwood Detected: Seeking Wychwood's Past in Today's Landscape

MARY WEBB

With a little detective work, Wychwood's past can still be uncovered in today's landscape.

At first glance, the modern landscape of the area seems to be much like that of many other parts of central England. The pleasant countryside has gently rolling hills and river valleys, and is predominantly agricultural with patches of woodland. There seems little link with the past history of the area and, with the exception of the Cornbury estate, few obvious traces of the vanished royal Forest and its inhabitants who lived and worked here. However, a closer look will reveal that this countryside is made up of many fragments from the past, which form a subtle framework for today's landscape, and may provide a guide for its future.

The modern landscape has evolved relatively recently, as a result of intensive and mechanised farming. Agriculture remained in the doldrums during the first half of the twentieth century, until the outbreak of the Second World War, which created the strategic need for home-grown food. Much land came under the plough, some for the first time. Subsequently, with the development of large-scale agricultural machinery over the last forty years, farming has changed from a labour-intensive activity to a food production industry. Many hedges have been removed and fields amalgamated to allow more efficient use of machinery. The ravages of Dutch elm disease in the 1970s have reduced dramatically the number of hedgerow trees, which previously gave a wooded appearance to much of the countryside. Modern arable farming practices mean that stubble and bare earth previously seen in the winter months are becoming unusual. Instead winter barley is sown in the autumn and is green throughout the winter. In summer, as well as cereals there are bright yellow expanses of oil seed rape, and recently the pale blue of linseed flowers. The impact of these changes sometimes seems so great as to obliterate all signs of the past, but, by looking carefully as you explore and get to know Wychwood, you will see that the present fieldscape is just another layer over the earlier landscape.

The Ordnance Survey Landranger 1:50 000 sheet 164 *Oxford* map is a good starting point from which to get an overall view. Notice the absence of villages in the large area surrounding the remnant of Wychwood Forest south-west of Charlbury. Some of the surrounding villages are clearly long-established and the churches, for example at Ascott-under-Wychwood, Shorthampton and Burford (on OS sheet 163), all have Norman work in their fabric. Nearer the Forest remnant, place names such as Leafield, Field Assarts and Asthall Leigh all suggest communities once in a woodland setting. On the very edge of the Forest remnant, names such as Kingstanding Farm and nearby Stag's Plain take us into the world of the royal hunting Forest. Similarly, the absence of villages in the swathe from Fulwell, near Enstone, south-east towards Bladon, passing through the estates of Ditchley and Blenheim, indicate another large area which was previously Forest woodland. Glympton Assarts Farm was clearly cut out of this woodland and some of the names of copses still remain, such as King's Wood and Deadman's Riding Wood.

FIELDS AND THEIR BOUNDARIES

Looking more closely at particular elements of today's landscape, perhaps the most obvious features are fields. Their shape and size can indicate something of their past. A good way to get an overview of the field patterns in the area is to look at the Ordnance Survey Explorer sheet 180 *Oxford* and the *Cotswolds* Outdoor Leisure 45 maps, both 1:25 000, covering the Wychwood area. Field boundaries are marked on these maps and shapes and sizes of fields can be clearly seen.

In the Wychwood area before enclosure, most cultivation was in the common, or open, field system with two, three or four large fields for each village. Often the names of these fields linger on, for example as Westfield and Eastfield. Beyond these common fields was an area of 'waste' – uncultivated ground – which was gradually encroached upon and brought into cultivation as the population expanded. Crops were rotated in the fields with one field lying fallow each year. These fields were divided into strips so that everyone had a share of the varying cultivated land. The fields were ploughed using heavy ploughs and oxen, the pattern of ploughing producing ridges which aided drainage. The ridges do not equate with the strips, which contained several such ridges. Today the remains of this ploughing system are evident as 'ridge-and-furrow'.

During the first half of the fourteenth century, a series of poor harvests and disease, culminating in the Black Death, led to a fall in population which in turn led to a change in farming practices. In some places sheep-grazed pasture replaced arable. Often the best ridge-and-

AN AERIAL
PHOTOGRAPH SHOWING
THE MEETING OF THE
UNPLANNED LANDSCAPE
OF ASSARTING AND THE
PLANNED LANDSCAPE
OF FOREST CLEARANCE
AND ENCLOSURE AT
LEAFIELD

furrow remains where this land has not since been ploughed, particularly on heavier land. These fields are often large and square in shape. There are examples near Shipton, south of the road towards Ascott-under-Wychwood.

Where open fields persisted, people gradually amalgamated their strips to make cultivation easier. With the permission of the Lord of the Manor, this land could be enclosed by hedges, made from woodland shrubs. Often long narrow fields were created, sometimes with a slight S shape, formed by the turning of the ox teams at the end of the amalgamated strips. There are examples of such fields between Charlbury and Spelsbury.

However, in most places enclosure of open fields took place in the seventeenth, eighteenth and nineteenth centuries, under acts of parliament. The declared aim was to improve methods of cultivation. The result was a radical change in the landscape, as well as the social structure of the agricultural community. The fields were laid out by surveyors and were usually quite large, rectangular in shape, and bounded by hawthorn hedges or stone walls. Typical examples of this 'planned countryside' can be seen in the Evenlode valley, above Chadlington. A similar regime of fields and farmsteads was also created north of Leafield, when much of the Forest was cleared in 1857.

In contrast to this planned countryside are the small irregularly shaped fields which were formed when woodland was gradually cleared over many centuries. Individuals often must have created fields by 'do-it-yourself' clearance, assisted by the grazing of animals. The results were small, asymmetrical, many-sided fields, with thick hedges formed by remnants of uncleared woodland. Sometimes these assarts were added to the open field system, or have been subsequently amalgamated, but their remains can nevertheless be seen, for example between North Leigh and Wilcote, and south of Leafield.

When woods were grubbed out to create fields, leaving their edges as field boundaries, it is sometimes possible to detect a 'ghost wood'. In ancient Wychwood, which contained many coppices, sometimes entire coppices were cleared, not necessarily all at once, leaving such a ghost. A good example is at Lee's Rest, east of Charlbury.

Hedges can clearly act as a clue to the origins of fields. Predominantly hawthorn hedges indicate fields made by Parliamentary enclosure; hedges with mixed species and woodland ground flora, such

91

WOOD ANEMONES AT
THE BASE OF AN
ANCIENT HEDGE

as yellow archangel and wood anemone, suggest hedges formed by woodland remnants around assart fields; and mixed hedges without woodland flora may be hedges created with shrubs taken from nearby woodland and planted on previously cultivated land. With time, the composition of a hedge develops as new species colonise. A rough rule of thumb is that in a thirty-metre length of hedge, each tree or shrub species which is present indicates a hundred years of development. But beware of the recent trend for planting mixed hedges – observe the age and shape of the shrubs as well as the number of species!

WOODLAND

Woodland can also give clues to the past. The remnant of Wychwood that lies to the south west of Cornbury is the largest area of broadleaved woodland in the region, but other smaller areas of similar woodland are sometimes as old and also have features which occur as a result of past woodland management.

The ancient names of woods and copses can still be seen on the Ordnance Survey maps for the area, not only around Cornbury and Ditchley, but also for example Stockley Copse, near Asthall Leigh, recorded in the Domesday survey and allocated to the king, and Coneygar Copse, meaning rabbit warren, near North Leigh. Historical research can tell us which are old and which are more recent, but field work can also assist.

The shapes of woods can reveal something of their past. Ancient wood boundaries often have irregular outlines, reflecting successive encroachments of farmland. The edges of Pinsley Wood, near Church Hanborough, and the north side of Cogges Wood are irregular and sinuous. In contrast, the edges of woods in planned countryside are often straight, coinciding with woodland rides, fences and ownership boundaries. North of Enstone, regular estate plantations are superimposed on the countryside. However, this distinction between planned and unplanned woodland is only very general and, for example, north-east of Leafield the ancient remnants of Wychwood have a straight edge marking the limit of the deforestation in 1857. Also, landscape designers have sometimes created sinuous outlines within their designs, to create a more natural effect. A local example of this is in parts of Eynsham Hall Park.

The structure of the individual woodlands can sometimes reveal their past. For example, in plantations trees were often planted in rows, but the absence of rows does not rule out planting. Equally, a plantation may contain earlier trees, and may occupy the site of a former ancient wood. Boynal Copse, south of Ascott-under-

Wychwood, is currently a conifer plantation, but occupies the site of a much older copse. The flora of woodland provides clues and woods with a long history often have a richer flora. However, unlike hedges, it is not possible to apply a rule of thumb assessing the age of a wood from the number of its species. There are certain ancient woodland indicator species, which in the Wychwood region include wood anemone, ramsons, yellow archangel, wood spurge and goldilocks buttercup. The wild service tree is strongly associated with ancient woodland, whereas nettles and elder suggest a site was once a field or dwelling.

Until about sixty years ago coppicing was a method used to grow

COPPICE ON A SHALLOW
WOOD BANK

wood for fencing posts, fuel and crafts such as hurdle-making. In this area hazel was the most commonly coppiced species. Hazel coppicing can be seen at the nature reserve at Foxholes, near Bruern, and there are many examples of neglected hazel coppice throughout Wychwood. In traditional woodmanship throughout England many broadleaved trees, besides hazel, were coppiced. As a result large stools developed, with the poles that sprouted from them being cropped in felling rotations of up to twenty-five years. Neglected coppice, with prominent stools, can be seen at Dean Grove near Spelsbury. Another variant was 'coppice with standards' , which was made up of even-aged coppice underwood, with an uneven-aged overstorey of 'standard' or large-size trees, often oak or ash, grown for timber to be used in the construction of buildings or ships.

Clearly, the sprouting coppice needed protection from grazing animals. In many ancient woodlands earth banks were created to act as a woodland edge. Sometimes these banks and ditches could be up to twenty-five feet in total width. A temporary fence would have been created on the bank, to keep grazing animals away from the young shoots of coppiced trees. An example of such a bank can be seen at Pinsley Wood near Church Hanborough.

Pollarding is the practice of cutting a tree between about six and fifteen feet above the ground, leaving a permanent trunk. Above this the tree sprouts in much the same way as a coppiced tree, but the shoots are above the reach of grazing animals. Pollarded trees are distinctive and were often used as boundary markers, as can be seen beside the southern boundary wall between Fordwells and Swinbrook, where the 'Oak Pollard' is the boundary of Asthall parish. In wood pastures, where the same piece of ground was used for trees and for grazing animals, pollarding kept the wood away from the grazing mouths below. In wood commons, local people had the right to pasture animals, with the trees belonging to the owner of the land. Such commons were a target for the enclosure movement but occasionally pollarded trees remain on former commons.

Sometimes the grazing animals were deer. At modern Blenheim the remains of wood pasture can be seen between High and Combe Lodge. The deer were probably kept in the park by a ditch, and pale or fence, the remains of which can still be made out between High and New Park towards the western edge of Blenheim. Sometimes such parks were simply utilitarian deer farms but at Woodstock Henry I built a hunting lodge in a wooded landscape, the precursor of the various landscape designs which can be studied at Blenheim. Similarly, ancient trees have survived at Cornbury, within the deer park.

THE 'OAK POLLARD' ON THE 'NEW ROAD' BETWEEN PAIN'S FARM, NEAR SWINBROOK, AND FORDWELLS. THIS OLD BOUNDARY MARKER WAS USED BY NINETEENTH-CENTURY SURVEYORS WHEN SETTING OUT NEW PARISH BOUNDARIES.

Banks can sometimes mark boundaries other than the edges of AN ANCIENT OAK IN
copses. The boundaries of parishes – which developed during Saxon THE PARK AT CORNBURY
times at least, and may even have their origins in Roman times or
before – were sometimes marked by banks, often surmounted by a
hedge. Examples can be seen running south east from Finstock.
Frequently parish boundaries follow the line of a stream, or may be
accompanied by an ancient path or road. Such banks should not be
confused locally with Grim's Ditch, which runs locally between
Ditchley and Woodstock.

VILLAGES, ROADWAYS AND HEATHS

The villages within Wychwood can tell us much about the past of
the countryside. As already mentioned, the ages of the churches are
significant. So too are other buildings. At Shipton and Enstone,
substantial tithe barns were built in the Middle Ages in these villages,
which lay beyond the woodland of the Forest. Within the wooded area
there were few such substantial buildings until the Victorians built, for
example, the powerful church of St Michael at Leafield, after the
enclosures. With the large-scale enclosure of the landscape to the north
and west of Leafield in 1857, when over two thousand acres (over eight
hundred hectares) of woodland were cleared, came model farms with

Victorian state-of-the-art buildings and mechanisation – for example at Fairspear and Kingstanding.

Sometimes villages were deserted. When the Black Death caused a drop in population some villages and hamlets became too small to survive and gradually fell into disrepair. Tangley, to the west of Bruern, was once considerably bigger than today, as was Chalford, to the west of Lidstone in the Glyme valley; and Tilgarsley, to the east of modern Eynsham Hall Park, ceased to exist altogether. In some places, bumpy ground, fairly regular patterns of rectangles showing the location of old houses, and clumps of nettles indicate the presence of a shrunken or, occasionally, deserted village.

The patterns of paths and roads also tell us something of the history of the landscape. Roman Akeman Street, running from St Albans to Cirencester, and the Salt Way, which passed Stonesfield and Chipping Norton on its way towards Droitwich, predate the medieval Forest. For much of their route through the Wychwood area, they have either become old green lanes, sometimes identified by field boundaries, or become lost completely only to be seen in crop marks from the air. With the creation of turnpike roads in the eighteenth century, where the tolls went towards the improvement and up-keep of the superior roads, many ancient routes deteriorated to little-used tracks and footpaths, and some have gone for ever.

Some old roads and paths meander around the edge of former assarts, especially in the area between North Leigh, Wilcote and

Ramsden. In contrast, the straight roads produced by the parliamentary enclosure acts of the eighteenth and nineteenth centuries stride across the countryside, for example radiating north-west of Chadlington and north-east of Stonesfield. Following the disafforestation of 1857, a new road was created between Fordwells and Swinbrook, along the line of an ancient open trackway, which had been part of the perambulation of the royal Forest at the time of King John. Like other 'new roads' this runs for nearly a mile with only a slight bend. This road is the boundary between Asthall and Leafield parishes and after 142 years locals still call this 'the new road'. Even within villages the enclosures made their mark, and at Shipton a new road, still so called, was created towards Upper Milton, and another towards Swinbrook.

THE ANCIENT SALTWAY

There were several heaths in the Wychwood area, the locations of which can be detected from place names, such as Ramsden Heath, Finstock Heath, Lyneham Heath Farm and several other Heath Farms throughout the area. Most disappeared with enclosure but one or two survived until as recently as the Second World War, when they were either put to cultivation or used for military encampments. Parts of Ramsden Heath were planted with conifers after the war. North Leigh Common still exists, a remnant of the extensive medieval Eynsham Heath. At Foxholes, parts of former Fifield Heath, with its more acidic soil, are now within the nature reserve.

By noticing often small-scale landscape features and underttanding their significance, the past use of the land can be glimpsed and the local character of the landscape more fully appreciated.

FURTHER READING

Bloxham, C., *Portrait of Oxfordshire*, 1982, Robert Hale.

Emery, F., *The Oxfordshire Landscape*, 1974, Hodder and Stoughton.

Schumer, B., *Wychwood – the Evolution of a Wooded Landscape*, 1999, The Wychwood Press.

Webb, M., Spicer, A. and Smith, A., *Oxfordshire Country Walks, Vol.1, Evenlode and Wychwood, 1990*, and *Vol. 5, Glyme Valley*, 1997, The Artisan Press.

7 The Wychwood Project

BELINDA FLITTER
& ALAN SPICER

Wychwood's landscape is rich and varied, with a fascinating history. It is an area of not one, but several, landscape characters with one Forest history. This common history has helped shape the landscape and its influences can be traced in many of the patterns and features which still exist today. In particular, as the preceding chapters show, the presence of the royal Forest and the restrictions of Forest law have had an impact on landscapes and habitats – not least on the amount and distribution of woodland, the mix of land uses, on patterns of settlement, land ownership and management. Remnants of the past – the ancient trees, woodland relic hedgerows, wood pasture, coppice, deer parks, wood boundaries and old routes through the Forest – can be found in many places throughout Wychwood. The existence of the Forest in the past has helped to make Wychwood the special place it is today.

Every landscape is the product of individual decisions made by a large number of landowners and managers. Usually those decisions are made for sound practical and economic reasons, often in response to new technology or changes in agricultural policy. However, unless we recognise that each of those individual decisions has an impact on the wider landscape, the features and patterns that give a landscape its special character can easily be lost, often simply because of a lack of appreciation of their significance.

The challenge for all of us who live and work in rural areas is to create a countryside for the future – a modern, economic, productive, attractive and sustainable countryside – without destroying the special character and historical identity of the area.

THE AIMS OF THE PROJECT

The Wychwood Project was established to encourage and support people living and working within the Wychwood area to take part in restoring the rich patchwork of landscapes and habitats that are so distinctive of the ancient Forest area.

The Project works in a number of ways: firstly, by raising awareness of the history and identity of the Forest area; secondly, by helping people to identify important habitats, locally distinctive features and landscape patterns; and then by helping people to develop plans for the conservation and restoration of these habitats, features and patterns wherever possible.

The aim is not to bring about a literal restoration of the medieval hunting Forest nor to preserve the present-day countryside in aspic: it is to encourage those with a stake in the area to work together to manage change in a very positive way. In doing so, it is hoped to strengthen people's sense of a local identity and their attachment to, and pride in, their local heritage.

The Project was conceived by local residents in 1995. Their idea was adopted by the Oxfordshire Nature Conservation Forum, a partnership of more than 50 authorities, agencies, organisations and individuals working for conservation in the county. It was seen as a means of achieving some of the objectives of the Oxfordshire Nature Conservation Strategy and as an important part of the county's work on Local Agenda 21. The Project was set up as an independent organisation operating under the auspices of the Oxfordshire Woodland Group, a registered charity. It was formally launched in 1997 with the opening of a new community woodland at Dean Common, near Chadlington.

The Project was chosen in 1998 by the North American/United Kingdom Countryside Exchange as a case study. Countryside experts from both sides of the Atlantic studied the Project in depth, and concluded that Wychwood was a special place, of national and international importance.

THE WYCHWOOD PROJECT'S vision is of the wide range of people living and working within the boundaries of the ancient royal hunting Forest of Wychwood contributing to the conservation and restoration of their local environment, to maintain a rich mosaic of farmland, settlements, woodland and other habitats. This will foster a sustainable, attractive, working landscape for the future which respects and builds upon the special character and history of the area.

AREA OF OPERATION

The Project operates within the Norman Wychwood Forest boundary which encompasses all or part of 41 modern parishes, and stretches from Burford in the west to Woodstock in the east, from Enstone in the north to the meeting place of the Windrush and the Thames in the south. The late medieval Forest area – centred on modern Blenheim, Cornbury, Ditchley and the area north of Witney, formerly Witney Chase – contains some of the largest remnants of the historic landscape, including ancient woodlands, wood pasture, limestone grassland, parkland, some fascinating old field systems, ancient hedgerows, former heaths, green lanes and ancient trees. This forms a priority area for the Project and has, arguably, the greatest scope for conservation and restoration. Beyond this core area, the emphasis is more on landscape enhancement and new habitat creation.

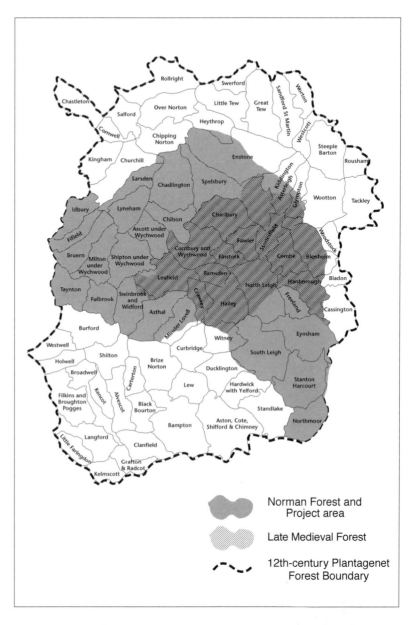

	Norman Forest and Project area
	Late Medieval Forest
	12th-century Plantagenet Forest Boundary

RAISING AWARENESS

Research carried out by Jane Corbett of University College London's Centre for Social and Economic Research on the Global Environment (CSERGE) in the Wychwood area suggests that local people do value the attractiveness of the Wychwood countryside but, as elsewhere, they are concerned about the loss of features such as stone walls and hedgerows and about the vitality and changing composition of its rural settlements. Many local residents are aware of the existence of the royal Forest, but few know just how big it used to be. Many are not aware of its legal meaning, denoting a royal hunting preserve, nor do they have much understanding of what the Forest might have looked like in the past. The term 'forest' today generally conjures up images of extensive areas of trees. Although the extent of woodland in the ancient Forest was greater than today, the area also had a variety of different, sometimes overlapping, land uses including settlements, arable land, common grazing land, parkland and heath.

The Wychwood Project offers a programme of talks, walks, displays and other events aimed at highlighting the special history and present-day character of the area. It encourages and helps people to find out more about the history of their particular part of the Wychwood and the changes that have taken place in the landscape over time. The Project is multi-dimensional, and appeals to a wide audience. Someone who may hesitate about their ability to identify species or habitats may be fascinated by local history and feel perfectly qualified to express

CSERGE carried out visitor surveys between 1997–9 at several Wychwood locations. These are a sample of some of the visitors' comments.

When I was a child living in the Forest I used to wander for miles. I loved the different kinds of flowers.

Leafield is an assart in the Forest, it's where the outlaws used to hang out.

We're privileged to be close to it. The connection with the past is important to me.

Children need to have ready access to the countryside to learn more about nature.

I'd like to see the woodlands we have... well conserved. But it's not likely there will be much expansion with the current agricultural policy.

Undo some of the things we did 40 years ago, when we straightened streams and drained wetland (retired farm manager).

Acquire woodland remnants. They need to be a minimum of 50 acres. You can't just rely on small communities planting here and there.

I would like to participate in the physical work of the project, for example scrub clearance, tree planting...

GUIDED WALKERS, LEARNING ABOUT WYCHWOOD

THE PROJECT OFFERS a 'menu' of parish-level initiatives, which includes

◆ Research into local landscape history

◆ Surveying and monitoring hedgerows, trees, birds and flowers

◆ Heritage tree schemes

◆ Parish trails and maps

◆ Practical conservation action, such as new tree planting and habitat restoration

◆ Creating community woodlands

their views about their local landscape. Others may be attracted to the Project through an interest in Wychwood's cultural heritage – the stories, legends and Forest lore.

For some, an understanding of history is an end in itself. Many find that a knowledge of the history of our landscape enables them to observe and appreciate it better. With this appreciation comes a sense of pride in the area, concern – and often action – for its conservation and restoration. An understanding of the changes that have taken place and the factors that have influenced those changes – for example economics, agricultural policy, advances in technology, patterns of ownership – can help us make informed choices about changes in the future. It can help us to identify important or characteristic features – such as ancient woodlands, woodland relic hedges, veteran trees, old field patterns, distinctive species or styles of management – and to identify what needs to be conserved, where improvements can be made and what opportunities exist for new habitats or particular landscape features.

The Project is community-based and there is no overall blueprint or master plan for the Wychwood area. Local people are encouraged to develop their own plans and their own shared vision for their part of the Forest. The Project acts as a catalyst and advises on practical conservation work arising out of this process.

This work can be carried out in a variety of ways – historical research or field-based surveys leading to reports, nature conservation plans, parish maps or trails. For example, a small group at Asthall Leigh and Fordwells which began simply with parish walks developed into a field boundary project. The resulting surveys are providing information for local farmers about the history, condition and species composition of their hedges and the state of their stone walls. A group in Charlbury undertook a Parish Conservation Plan (PCP), which included detailed hedge surveys and led to the creation of local nature reserves in the town.

PCPs are a countywide initiative and identify key habitats and important landscapes across a parish. This information is summarised in a report and a series of annotated plans. These can then be used by parish councils and other community groups to identify, prioritise and plan practical conservation activity. The results can also stimulate local landowners to take another look at their part of the parish and to implement restoration projects of their own. Field surveys undertaken can often highlight the good work that farmers have already done and, if these surveys are repeated over time, they can show increases in wildlife due to new planting or changes in management.

The Project works with individual farmers, researching the history of the farm and identifying key features for conservation including any ancient woodland, woodland relic hedges, veteran trees, ancient field patterns, old meadows and archaeological features. Research can highlight features which have been lost and opportunities for restoration. The information can be used to improve The Farming and Wildlife Advisory Group's (FWAG) Whole Farm Conservation Plans and to support grant applications.

An interesting case study is that of Glebe Farm, Freeland. Here the Project has helped identify ancient woodland, and woodland relic hedges with their wiggly edges and hedge banks. The ancient field boundary system is being restored and field margins created to protect important hedgerows and old pollarded oaks.

One of the beneficial spin-offs of all this work is that a lot of very detailed research is being done into history, landscapes and habitats in the area. This is potentially a marvellous resource and the Project is trying to bring it together and make it publicly accessible. The new Woodlands Gallery in the County Museum at Woodstock may be an important outlet for some of this material. The Project also offers many educational opportunities for students of all ages. North Leigh Primary School has acquired its own area of woodland which adjoins the school and was formerly part of North Leigh Heath. It contains relics of old hedgerow and over thirty different species of trees and shrubs as well as many other plants and animals. The wood is used to help teach history

LEFT: YOUNG FORESTERS CLEARING DEBRIS FROM THEIR NEWLY ACQUIRED WOOD AT NORTH LEIGH SCHOOL

RIGHT: A GLIMPSE OF THE WOODLAND AT NORTH LEIGH SCHOOL

and ecology, and the pupils manage it as their contribution to the Project. The University of Reading's Geography Department has helped the Project to produce a digital data-base of Wychwood's landscape and habitats.

CONSERVING AND RESTORING LANDSCAPES AND HABITATS

The Project provides technical advice and support for practical conservation and restoration projects. It helps with funding applications and tries to attract into the project area additional finance for such work.

A wide range of farm-based restoration work is now underway, including hedgerow and tree planting, dry stone walling and management of scrub and grassland. The Project brings in specialist advice and also organises volunteer tasks where necessary. It also highlights good practice through farm visits and other events.

A community group at Leafield decided that they wanted each child in the village to be able to plant a tree for the Millennium. The Project organised training both for the children and the adults on collecting and growing trees from seed. Several hundred native tree seeds were collected locally and grown. The group has now found a site, with help

GAPS FILLED IN A HEDGEROW AND HEDGEROW TREES PLANTED, BETWEEN DITCHLEY AND SPELSBURY

from the Project, where these trees will soon be planted to help create a community woodland. Children from Leafield Primary School have also helped plant a large number of trees as part of a landscaping scheme being carried out by TWR near Leafield.

West Oxfordshire District Council owns a piece of rough,

TOP: VOLUNTEER STONE-WALLERS

MIDDLE: A HEDGE RECENTLY LAYED BY VOLUNTEERS NEAR CATSHAM BRIDGE, CHADLINGTON

BOTTOM: YOUNG ASSISTANTS AT LEAFIELD'S TREE NURSERY

105

The Project supports FWAG's Whole Farm Approach to conservation on the farm, in which specialised habitat management is integrated into day-to-day farming operations. FWAG is strong in Oxfordshire, and West Oxfordshire District Council is currently offering additional funding for farmers in the Project area to commission Whole Farm Conservation Plans from FWAG. These plans provide a concise working document and management schedule which enable farmers and landowners to become involved in practical action on nature conservation. The Project works alongside organisations such as FWAG to ensure that their advisers understand the historical context in which they operate.

overgrown common ground near North Leigh, known as North Leigh Heath or North Leigh Common. Once part of a much larger heath stretching from near Witney to Eynsham, this area is now being restored by the council with the support and encouragement of the Project. A management plan has been drawn up and the local community will take part in the restoration. More information about this restoration is given at page 128.

WOODLAND PLANTING AND MANAGEMENT

Woodland is clearly a key habitat within the ancient Forest area. In spite of the clearances, very significant areas of woodland remain, particularly associated with some of the major country estates. The woodland remnant nowadays known as Wychwood Forest, lying to the south-west of Charlbury, covers 870 hectares (2150 acres) and is the largest continuous area of ancient woodland in Oxfordshire. Beyond this central area there are several very substantial blocks and a scatter of smaller isolated woodlands which are also fragments of the ancient Forest's woodland.

The Project is encouraging landowners to replace some of the woodland cover that has been lost within the area and to ensure that those woodlands which are left are actively managed. It aims in particular to extend existing woods which are often too small to be viable either economically or for wildlife. It aims to create links between remaining woodland fragments where possible, either with new planting or with other wildlife habitat corridors, to create a patchwork of carefully sited new woodlands across the area. The Project has a target of creating 800 hectares of new woodland by 2009. The majority of these new woodlands will be privately owned and managed but parish groups are encouraged to contribute by establishing community woodlands. In its first two years the Project gave advice on the creation of 28 hectares (about 70 acres) of new woodland, and helped establish four community woodlands.

An excellent example of private local woodland planting has taken place recently near Fairspear House, overlooking the Evenlode valley between Leafield and Shipton. Here two adjoining owners have, with the advice and assistance of the Wychwood Project, together created 2.5 hectares (about 6 acres) of woodland. Predominantly oak and ash have been planted, with smaller trees including field maple, wild service and hazel for coppicing. Shrubs planted include buckthorn, guelder rose and spindleberry. Landscape improvement and the encouragement of wildlife are the principal aims of this unified design.

Lee's Rest Farm, near Charlbury, was originally part of Lee's Rest

LEFT: TREE PLANTING NEAR FAIRSPEAR HOUSE

RIGHT: REVIVED WOODLANDS AND POND AT LEE'S REST, CHARLBURY

LEFT: PART OF DEAN COMMON, PLANTED IN 1997

RIGHT: H.M. LORD LIEUTENANT FOR OXFORDSHIRE, HUGO BRUNNER, AND HIS DEPUTY, MALCOLM COCHRANE, HELPING PLANT A COMMUNITY WOOD BETWEEN SHIPTON AND MILTON-UNDER-WYCHWOOD

Wood, an ancient Wychwood woodland most of which was finally cleared in 1857. Recently, with the guidance and assistance of the Oxfordshire Woodland Project, three woodlands totalling 4 hectares (about 10 acres) on previously neglected woodland sites have been replanted and a large pond restored.

At Dean Common, instead of landfilling an old 8-hectare (about 20 acre) sand and gravel pit, Hanson plc., working with the Project and Oxfordshire County Council, have created a community woodland. Nearly 9000 native trees and shrubs typical of ancient Wychwood have been planted, leaving broad grassy rides and glades either side of the Oxfordshire Way public bridleway, with wetland and other habitats being created as well. The edges of the woodland have been designed to create sheltered environments to encourage invertebrates including indigenous woodland butterflies like the grizzled skipper, and eventually the Duke of Burgundy and the white admiral. Areas of the rides have been seeded with appropriate wild flora. An existing pond has been enlarged and marginal wet areas created, with new hedgerows planted to control access to those parts of the common most beneficial to wildlife.

The parishes of Milton, Shipton and Ascott-under-Wychwood have worked together with the Project and The Woodland Trust to create a community wood at Shipton, which will link existing woodland and another recently planted area to create a substantial block of woodland — in all nearly a kilometre in length – on the edge of the village.

BUILDING PARTNERSHIPS

The Project operates as an umbrella organisation for all of these activities. It also acts as a catalyst and co-ordinates and supports action across the area. For the Project to achieve what it has set out to do, it needs to build partnerships between everyone living and working within the area — agencies, authorities, organisations, businesses and all sectors of the community, particularly those responsible for managing land. Rarely do these different groups and individuals have entirely the same objectives. Local residents want to be able to enjoy the surrounding countryside and are often concerned by the apparent loss of hedgerows and other features. Landowners often express the desire to take part in conserving wildlife in the area, but operate under a wide and complex range of economic, policy and practical constraints. Many would like to take up available grants but are concerned that they may have to provide public access in the future. The Project supports public access by agreement, but also aims to conserve and extend existing habitats, and care must be taken not to destroy these habitats by inappropriate change. The Project acts as a forum for discussion, to ensure that everyone is working together to achieve the best for Wychwood in the long term.

FRIENDS OF WYCHWOOD

Any individual or organisation supporting the aims of the Project can become a Friend of Wychwood. As well as acting as a voice for the area, Friends are encouraged to feed ideas and views into the Project as a whole and to become involved in the Project's local activities, including fundraising. Working together, the Project and the Friends offer a programme of walks, visits, practical conservation activities and talks, and produce a quarterly newsletter, *Forest Update*. The Project has a web site which can be visited at www.wychwoodproject.org

Wychwood landowners

Vicky Price of Woodstock has carried out a study of landowners' views within the Wychwood area. These are a some of her initial findings.

The Wychwood Project area has a wide range of landowners, from those owning a few hectares, to estates with a few thousand. A common factor linking this diverse range of owners is their love of the area they live in, look after and in many cases make their living from. Many desire not only to keep the countryside as it is, but to 'put something back' for future generations. Most farmers do see conservation as good practice and the way that land should be managed. This is illustrated by the wide range of conservation schemes that are currently being undertaken in the area, from building otter holts to hedgerow restoration, from tree planting to the creation of field margins. The dominance of woodland creation and planting indicates the bias of local estates towards forestry enterprises. This is partly due to all the estates running commercial shoots with the corresponding need for cover, but parkland restoration also indicates conservation as a prime aim.

These measures are all part of the schemes which the Wychwood Project aims to promote, such as the Farm Woodland Grant Scheme, the Upper Thames Tributaries Environmentally Sensitive Area, Whole Farm Plans and Countryside Stewardship.

Financial interests are obviously important in most cases with many owners making their living from the land. Many areas of land which are in the various schemes are those of poorer quality, and it is often these that have the greatest ecological value. Landowners express amazement at the diversity and speed of return of organisms that recolonise when conservation measures are adopted. To quote one farmer, talking about some permanent set-aside, 'the wildlife has gone back to how it used to be when I was a boy'. However, many farmers cannot see how the current levels of grants for conservation schemes will provide them with a living. These grants can contribute towards income, but will not solely support a farm.

Agriculture is continually shaping the landscape. Farmers perceive that the picking of a date from the Forest's history, a date when there was no mechanisation and a lower population, was 'not to be moving with the times'. Also, in the eastern parishes of the Project area there are large areas of woodland which were cited as being part of the area's special character. These woodlands are already being expanded. Clearly there is a need to look at what is already there. The majority of farmers considered that they were already doing what the Project wanted to achieve, and thought this should be taken into account when the Project decided its priorities. In many cases history, rather than topography, was seen to govern how an area was farmed, which is important if historically-based schemes are to be promoted locally.

Farmers and landowners are the people who will help achieve the aims of trying to restore landscape and habitats. The Project needs to explain to farmers what it is trying to achieve without giving the impression that farmers are being told how to farm their land. The aim of creating a rich and varied landscape by improving what already exists should be promoted rather than, say, specific tree-planting targets.

From the perspective of farmers and landowners, there is potential for the Wychwood Project to be a successful community conservation project, provide it is marketed properly with clear and accurate information. It also needs sound financial backing which can provide additional contributions to existing grant schemes available in the area.

Elements of Wychwood's landscape: fostering character and wildlife

CHARLES KEIGHLEY
& NICK DALBY

During a long period of its history Wychwood was managed as a royal hunting Forest. As a result, today's landscape is often rich, diverse and distinctive. This landscape is built up of many elements, some large, like areas of woodland and arable fields, some small, like roadside verges and Cotswold stone walls, and many in between like the houses and gardens we live in and the trees which grow around our villages. Altogether they create that mosaic which makes up Wychwood's fine countryside.

This countryside is a product of human and physical influences, which together create its characteristic features. It continually evolves and changes. Sometimes the changes take place over a prolonged period of time, for example the regeneration of woodland at the end of Roman rule; sometimes the changes are dramatic, for example the nineteenth-century woodland clearances. At other times the changes are piecemeal, often only becoming apparent in retrospect. Nowadays the changes brought about by modern agriculture, especially in the last few decades, are well publicised; but there are also threats to the essentially rural character of Wychwood's villages and small towns from demographic changes and improvements in communications, especially by road. Gradual 'suburbanisation' – with unnecessary street lights, concrete kerb stones, tarmacadammed lanes and excessively mown verges – is often eroding the distinct character of the local landscape.

A knowledge of local history can influence future management of the landscape. By researching the history, ecology and character of the landscape, it is often possible to give priority to certain conservation work in order to safeguard and enhance those elements of most value and potential for improvement.

This chapter highlights some of the features of Wychwood's landscape which can be maintained and enhanced, often with benefits for wildlife. We hope these simple suggestions may also help those who live and work in the Wychwood area to strengthen the existing character of the area's landscape. Often attention to detail – not just what we do, but the way that we do it – is important. The results will not only be a visual improvement, but will also help control pollution, assist the rural economy and create more diverse local habitats.

WOODLANDS

Much of Wychwood's woodland remains, as a result of the stewardship of the larger local estates, especially Cornbury, Blenheim and Ditchley as well as several others, for example at Swinbrook, Bruern, Kiddington and Eynsham Hall. Clearly the preservation of existing woodlands is visually important in the landscape. But there are other vital reasons, more difficult to perceive at the local level, such as fixing carbon dioxide emissions and maintaining biodiversity. Like equatorial rain-forests globally, our woodlands are often vital locally.

Some existing woodland is ecologically more valuable than others. Ancient woodland – woodland which is more than 400 years old – is an irreplaceable natural asset. Locally such woods include Holly Grove, Dean Grove, Pinsley Wood and Tar Wood as well as much woodland associated with the principal estates. The value of any new woodland for nature conservation is increased if it is planted next to such ancient or species-rich woodland. In the longer term the sum of the two woods together will be greater than their parts.

Often the perception of woodland cover can be increased with only a small proportion of the land being planted with trees and the remainder in agricultural use. For example new planting on higher ground often has greater visual effect, increasing the overall height of the woodlands in the landscape and contrasting with the valleys below. Good examples of this are the existing woodlands around Ranger's

A LANDSCAPE OF COPSES: LOOKING NORTH FROM NEAR ASTHALL BARROW ACROSS THE WINDRUSH VALLEY TOWARDS WIDLEY COPSE, FAWS GROVE AND PART OF HENS GROVE

Lodge, north of Cornbury, and the woodlands above Fulbrook, north-east of Burford. Also, well designed belts of woodland can have an impact similar to that of much larger blocks of woodland.

Beryl Schumer has described the substantial copses which contributed to the medieval Forest's landscape. Many have been cleared but many still exist. Often they are still fundamental elements in Wychwood's landscape, and may provide a foundation on which to build.

In some cases, a former copse has been partially cleared, leaving woodland from which runs a hedgerow or wood bank marking the former boundary. An example of this can be seen at Cranehill Copse, west of Charlbury. Sometimes a former copse has been fully cleared, leaving only an ancient hedgerow to mark the outline of the woodland, for example at Lee's Rest, east of Charlbury. New planting can respect these ancient boundaries, and even if the copse is to be only partially replanted, the effect of substantial woodland can still be created by extending the former boundary to create a belt of woodland on the perimeter of the copse.

Some ancient copses remain, but have been planted with conifers. Despite this replanting, the flora and fauna at the site may still be significant, especially around the edges. Incentives exist for such conifer plantations to be replaced, as they are felled, with appropriate broadleaved trees. Recent clearances of conifers in the Wychwood area have allowed swathes of dormant woodland plants, including ancient woodland indicators such as yellow archangel, wood anemone and primrose, to regenerate in response to sunlight.

A SMALL WOOD ON THE BROW OF THE HILL ABOVE PUDLICOTE. SUCH WOODS ARE OFTEN WORTH SYMPATHETIC ENLARGEMENT, TO BENEFIT WILDLIFE AND INCREASE THEIR IMPACT IN THE LANDSCAPE.

SITING WOODS

- It is always worth seeking professional advice. There are many considerations, in what is a significant investment. Think and plan carefully before you decide to plant. Woodland planting is a long-term activity. Getting it right from the outset will save time and money.

- Specialist advice about the local landscape, its history and ecology is readily available. These topics should be high on the agenda. Often forestry professionals can themselves seek specialist advice on these, as well as on the visual aspects of landscape design. Sources of advice are given at the end of this chapter.

- Conduct your own research – it is often rewarding and informative to know the history of a site and its surroundings. Fascinating information is readily available. Always try to avoid destroying something else on the site which may be of greater value. Much of Wychwood lies within the Cotswold Area of Outstanding Natural Beauty, and the AONB have carried out an historic landscape assessment. West Oxfordshire District Council has published a detailed and comprehensive landscape assessment of the whole district, including Wychwood. Much of Wychwood lies within the Upper Thames Tributaries Environmentally Sensitive Area, and the ESA has been carefully assessed. Oxfordshire County Council has produced an 'alert' map of ecologically significant sites. English Nature has a register of ancient woodlands over 2 hectares and local information can be obtained on smaller woods .

- The siting of woodland should be seen as part of the bigger picture, in the pattern of the whole landscape. How can the woodland link with characteristic elements in this wider landscape?

There has to be a place in the landscape for more commercially viable softwoods, but care needs to be taken with the siting of such plantations. It is often possible to soften their impact, for example by planting a perimeter of broadleaved trees. The Forestry Commission has demonstrated, at the Wyre Forest near Kidderminster, how such commercial woodland can be made attractive. Advice on landscape design is readily available when planting such woodlands.

Between the larger areas of existing woodland, and often along the valley sides, are smaller areas of woodland. These may for example be remnants from early assarting (clearance of woodland for agriculture) or later shelter belts and game coverts. Where assarting has taken place, woodland remnants and hedgerows may have survived from ancient woodland and may be species-rich. Such ancient woods under 2 hectares are not recorded in English Nature's inventory of ancient woodland, but are still of significant value. Like larger areas of woodland, these smaller woods are often ideal for sympathetic enlargement.

The pattern of nearby field boundaries is often significant and tree planting can reflect existing boundaries. For example, a straight woodland boundary would look out of place in the unplanned landscape of irregularly shaped fields which have been created by assarting. In the case of smaller such fields, it may even be possible to plant the whole field, thus creating a new wood which coincides exactly with the surrounding field boundaries and ancient hedges. Similarly, irregular planting can look out of place in planned fields created by the enclosures, where straight blocks of planting may be more appropriate. The scale of the landscape and local topography need to be carefully considered at every site.

The selection of species to be planted will depend upon soil type, aspect, location and the objectives of the land owner. It is worth seeking advice, whatever the scale of planting. Inappropriate trees can lead to the suburbanisation of the countryside and dilute the essential local character. Wychwood has a wide range of indigenous species of trees and shrubs which can be considered, with different species being characteristic of particular locations. It is worth investigating what is already growing in the vicinity, to differentiate between what has been planted and what is growing naturally. Once the basic natural species have been ascertained, they are best planted simply, avoiding unnecessarily complicated mixtures.

Especially in smaller new woods with conservation a prime aim, the use of locally sourced seedlings is advisable, to encourage and preserve genetic purity. A woodland field layer of flowering plants will be encouraged by rotational coppicing.

Some sites will not be suitable for planting trees. Land managers are often tempted to plant trees in those areas which are simply difficult to cultivate – where the combine harvester will not reach – but often these sites are ecologically important in their own right, for example containing limestone grassland or areas of scarce marshland. It is important to carry out research before making planting decisions.

Generally the smaller and younger a tree is when planted, the quicker it will become established. Often it is tempting to plant expensive larger trees, but these are less likely to thrive, and in the longer term will be surpassed by smaller trees planted at the same time. November and February are usually the best months to plant broadleaves. Once planted, trees need monitoring and replacing where necessary. Fencing, pest and weed control always need to be considered. Research by the National Trust after the gales of 1987 suggests that on sites that have already been wooded natural regeneration may be a quicker method than planting to re-establish woodland. In certain locations in Wychwood, and especially in woods with nature conservation as their prime aim, natural regeneration could be allowed to occur.

POPULAR SMALL
WOODLAND OBJECTIVES

- Enhance landscape value
- Improve nature conservation
- Produce marketable timber
- Screen unsitely features
- Provide shelter for buildings and livestock
- Enhance sporting value

DEER HAVE DESTROYED THIS SAPLING. JUST AS IN PREVIOUS TIMES, DEER CONTROL AND APPROPRIATE GUARDS ARE ESSENTIAL.

The management of existing woodland also has an impact on the landscape and nature conservation. Landowners increasingly aim for more sensitive forms of management, rather than simply going for the cheapest in the short term. The visual impact of clear felling should be avoided if possible, with uneven aged forestry within managed systems being pursued instead. Coppicing and coppice with standards should be considered. Some old woodland should be left 'unmanaged', and in other woodland ancient trees and dead wood – both of which provide excellent habitats for birds, insects and lower plants such as lichens, fungi and mosses – should remain.

GREEN LINKS, FIELD BOUNDARIES AND MARGINS

Links can be created between areas of woodland, both large and small. These links not only create the visual effect of substantial woodland, but also create conservation corridors spreading from ancient woodlands throughout the surrounding landscape. If well planted such links can, in cross-section, contain a field layer of flowering plants, a shrub layer, smaller trees and a core of forest trees, all typical of Wychwood, thus creating the effect of woodland in a fairly narrow strip of land. Grants are often available for such work.

In the nineteenth century shelter belts of Scots pines were sometimes planted in Wychwood, especially in areas which had recently been enclosed, and these have become something of a local feature. These belts are sometimes worth maintaining and replanting to strengthen local character, despite not being indigenous species.

Individual hedgerow trees are also important landscape features and

TREES AND SHRUBS
TYPICAL OF WYCHWOOD

• Larger trees – oak and ash.

• Smaller trees – field maple, the wild service tree, hazel and holly.

• Shrubs – the wayfaring tree, spindleberry, midland hawthorn, blackthorn and dogwood.

contribute to green links between areas of woodland. They are important for many species of birds, bats and insects. If the hedgerow is itself ancient, or if it links ancient or species-rich woodland, these trees will be particularly important for wildlife. Many disappeared with Dutch elm disease. Careful hedge trimming can allow trees, typically oak and ash in Wychwood, to grow above the hedgerow. Such hedgerow trees in hedges running north-south are less likely to shade adjacent crops than those growing east-west.

If hedgerow trees are allowed to develop on both sides of a country road, an informal avenue is created. An example can be seen along the road between Enstone and Taston. If the trees become particularly close and dense, they can create almost a tunnel of trees. In general, planted formal avenues are only suitable for baroque landscapes, for example at Blenheim and parts of Cornbury, and look out of place in the more informal open countryside.

Gradually, as green links are created between larger and smaller areas of woodland, hedgerow trees extend these links into the farmed landscape.

Field boundaries and the margins associated with them are important in the landscape. Often they have a significant visual impact, and they are also important to wildlife, both in their own right as well as providing corridors which allow wildlife, both animals and plants, to move and eventually colonise from one place to another. These boundaries and margins are the basic link in the green network. They require management, and farmers often give them, as well as their crops, care and attention. Such boundaries can be managed in

117

conjunction with adjacent habitats, even if these happen to lie beyond the legal limits of the farm.

Hedges are important features in Wychwood's landscape. The Hedgerow Regulations of 1997 were introduced to protect the most valuable hedgerows from destruction, including irreplaceable ancient hedgerows and those which are recognised nationally as being very important to the landscape. However, many are not protected and hedgerows continue to be in decline. Fortunately many of Wychwood's hedgerows have survived, but some are gappy and poorly maintained. They can be restored by coppicing, or by laying which is less drastic to wildlife. Sometimes gaps need replanting with appropriate native species. Occasionally it may be possible to plant entirely new hedges, to break up extremely large fields.

Once restored, hedgerows have to be maintained. Sometimes they can be allowed to grow free, and can be cut on a long cycle of between five and ten years. This balance of tall growth with a denser base provides an excellent habitat, especially if cut in rotation around the farm and in association with neighbouring farmers. Sometimes hedges can be trimmed more often, preferably not annually but every second or third year so as to ensure food supplies for wildlife in intervening years. Trimming on alternate sides, rather than both sides at once, can also benefit wildlife. These more frequently trimmed hedges should be about 2 metres high. Hedge junctions are particularly favoured by songbirds and, where there is no conflict with cropping, can be allowed

GREEN LINKS IN THE LANDSCAPE: THE EVENLODE VALLEY BETWEEN CORNBURY AND SPELSBURY

freer growth. Hedges should not be cut between the beginning of April and the end of August, when cutting will be harmful to invertebrates and breeding birds. Some hedges can be left untrimmed through the autumn to provide a supply of ripened berries and fruits. Selected saplings can be tagged and left during trimming, to allow them to develop into hedgerow trees.

Cotswold stone walls are important elements in some of Wychwood's landscape, and have been so since at least the parliamentary enclosures. As well as looking attractive, walls provide shelter and protect adjacent habitats. Lichens and moss grow on them and birds, insects, small mammals, amphibians and reptiles take cover there. Sadly, many local stone walls have become gappy and broken down. Nowadays they are expensive to repair, but grants and volunteers can often help with this. Resources can be devoted to maintaining those walls which have the most visual impact, for example along roadways, footpaths and near to villages.

Fences can be significant in the landscape, especially if correctly placed and well maintained. Traditional post and rail fences may be appropriate, especially near villages and farmsteads. The siting of fences can be of significance to wildlife, and should be at least a metre away from the edge of the field to provide a small but valuable area for wildlife.

In the past limestone grasslands, associated with sheep runs, were an important and species-rich local habitat. Some modern farming

A WELL-MAINTAINED FIELD MARGIN, WHICH PROVIDES ESSENTIAL HABITAT FOR WILDLIFE SUCH AS THE FORAGING BARN OWL WHILST SUPPRESSING ANNUAL WEEDS

methods and incentives have led to a decline in grassland, as well as hedgerows and associated trees, with a consequent decline in dependent species. This loss of species can be reversed by incorporating quite simple measures, often relating to field margins, into modern farming practice. The Farming and Wildlife Advisory Group (FWAG) are leaders in providing guidance to enable farmers to reconcile viable farming with landscape and nature conservation.

For example, many existing hedge bottoms and field edges have received herbicide and fertiliser, resulting in an unstable and species-poor plant community of limited attraction to wildlife. Circumstances vary, and FWAG provide professional advice on the best approach to create a stable community, attractive to wild life, without threatening crop yields. Once stabilised, FWAG recommend arable field margins with a 2 metre strip of grass kept coarse, beyond which lies a 4 metre strip of grass cut annually. This field margin will provide essential habitat for wild life, for example the foraging barn owl, whilst suppressing annual weeds. Foxgloves, vetches, bumblebees, butterflies and yellowhammers are typical species which will benefit from such margins. These margins also allow hedge trimming to take place more easily in late autumn, when cultivated land would be compacted and damaged by heavy machinery. This wildlife habitat can be extended by creating a 'conservation headland' in the outer 6 metres of the crop where only selective pesticides are used.

Arable stubble and other crop residues which are allowed to remain throughout the autumn and winter greatly benefit many farmland birds which sadly are now in decline. Similarly uncultivated field corners, crops planted for the shelter and feeding of game birds, and set-aside land will aid the survival of many once common birds such as the corn bunting, grey partridge, bullfinch and linnet.

Where it still survives, unimproved grassland is an important habitat, especially for wild flowers and insects. It is becoming rare in Wychwood. With the benefit of Countryside Stewardship grants, grazing management can be reintroduced to preserve and extend these fragile habitats. Wychwood is a target area for Countryside Stewardship. Set-aside, if it continues, can be used as a buffer between arable land and wildlife habitats, including unimproved grassland as well as woodland and meadows.

Scrub margins are an important habitat for many forms of wildlife, particularly many song birds, and can be a positive conservation measure. Instead of being regarded as unwanted and untidy, scrub can sometimes be allowed to develop and grow, especially at margins adjacent to woodland.

CHURCH HANBOROUGH, AT THE
EASTERN EXTREMITY OF
WYCHWOOD. NEARBY IS ANCIENT
PINSLEY WOOD.

VILLAGES

Wychwood's villages are fundamental to the landscape, tucked into the valleys or standing high on the limestone uplands. All provide opportunities for strengthening the character of the landscape and for habitat creation.

The distinction between settlement and surrounding countryside is visually particularly important in the Wychwood landscape. Sometimes boundaries are becoming blurred, especially where ribbon development, over-grazed equestrian paddocks and short-life buildings intrude into the open countryside. How can the distinctive features of our villages be strengthened?

The entrances to individual villages are often important, and can be marked by tree planting to distinguish the community from the

OLD ORCHARDS NEAR
UPPER FARM, RAMSDEN surrounding, often arable, countryside. Several local towns and villages are already creating community woods. If well designed, these woods can provide for recreation and be places where local children can learn about nature. Such woods can benefit wildlife and complement the local landscape, and if well sited can also often act as a boundary to the village. Within the villages, local greens, sports fields, recreation grounds and verges often cry out for trees to be planted or replaced.

Indigenous trees typical of Wychwood are usually most appropriate for village planting. Sometimes other trees may be suitable, for example horse chestnut on a village green, or a specimen larch to provide individuality and grace. Robust trees are always best for public places. Occasionally a particular type of tree is associated with a particular village, for example Shipton-under-Wychwood has many lime trees, planted by earlier owners of Shipton Court.

Gardens, paddocks and smallholdings are important components in the village landscape and can become rich habitats, especially for birds. They provide excellent opportunities to plant the smaller trees and shrubs associated with Wychwood, for example wild cherry, crab apple, hawthorn, wild service, holly and field maple. Orchards sadly have declined, and owners of paddocks around the villages may consider planting fruit trees, wherever possible on full standard stems.

Ornamental trees are better reserved for gardens. If a tree has to be felled, it is often worth leaving some dead wood to provide a habitat for insects and birds.

Boundary walls, fences and hedgerows are important components of the village landscape, and often have a public face. Before erecting a new boundary structure or altering an existing one, consider carefully what is appropriate to the location, in order to conserve and strengthen the overall character of the village. In many Wychwood villages dry stone walls predominate. Elsewhere hedges are appropriate, especially of native species, sometimes mixed. If evergreens are required, plant native holly or yew, rather than the ubiquitous leyland cyprus.

New buildings are often created in our communities, and their impact on the surroundings can be mitigated and softened by appropriate planting.

Verges and open spaces in and around villages are potentially important habitats. Natural borders, beneficial to wildlife, can be created simply by leaving some longer grasses and wild flowers which are cut annually in the autumn, adjacent to shorter grass and lawns which are cut more often. This is especially true of road side verges, and such a policy may reduce maintenance costs.

Last but not least, we should treasure our churchyards, which are

123

often delightful combinations of buildings, sculpture and vegetation. Their dry stone walls, trees, shrubberies and grassland usually provide nest sites, cover, food stores and nectar for insects and many kinds of wildlife. The designation of areas of grassland, away from paths and frequently visited graves, will create spring and summer flowering meadows which provide valuable habitats.

POLLARDED WILLOWS NEAR ASCOTT-UNDER-WYCHWOOD

WATERCOURSES, MEADOWS AND PONDS

Streams, rivers and meadows are important features in Wychwood's landscape, and in the past so were ponds. Often they create a particular impact when near or within towns and villages.

Many streams rise from springs on the valley sides, and flow down to the three rivers which intersect Wychwood. Sometimes the fields in which they are located have been drained, and occasionally the streams have been put in culverts, with a resulting loss of habitat. Trees can be retained around these streams, provided they do not cause excessive shading, and boggy margins encouraged where plants such as marsh marigold, ragged robin and yellow iris can thrive.

The rivers and their margins provide good habitats for birds, plants, mammals, invertebrates and fish. With proper management even the reclusive otter may return. Owners and managers of riverside land should always discuss maintenance and improvement works with the Environment Agency before any work is undertaken. The temptation to remove pools and meanders should be avoided. Generally, fences standing well away from the edge of the watercourse prevent excessive erosion from grazing stock. Marginal riverside plants can be retained, on at least one side of the river, and can be cleared by rotation every 5 to 7 years. Some tree planting may be appropriate, with suitable species such as alder and crack willow. If willows are pollarded, a rotation has to be followed, with pollarding work being carried out during autumn and winter to minimise disturbance to wildlife. Fertilisers and pesticides should not be used within at least 10 metres of the river margins.

Traditional meadows in the flat land alongside the rivers have long

124

TRADITIONAL MEADOWS
NEAR SHORTHAMPTON,
WITH WYCHWOOD ON
THE HORIZON

been a part of the Wychwood landscape. Often these grasslands have high wildlife value, especially if they have not been re-seeded or cultivated. Nowadays many come within the Upper Thames Environmentally Sensitive Area (ESA) and are eligible for additional grants if traditional grazing patterns are pursued. As well as the great burnet, cuckoo flower, orchids and other attractive flowers, birds such as the snipe, lapwing and redshank benefit from these meadows.

In very low-lying land, between the lower Windrush and the Thames, it may be possible to create a wet wood, full of willows and alder. This habitat, in effect a flood plain forest, has ceased to exist in England but must have existed in Wychwood before marshland was drained and river banks were cleared. Such a forest was the natural habitat of the black poplar, Britain's rarest timber tree.

ONE OF WILCOTE'S
MANY PONDS

There are a considerable number of ponds and former ponds in Wychwood, vital habitats for many creatures and plants, including frogs, reed buntings, dragonflies and various sedges. They are oases of shallow water wetlands, and all are all worth surveying. Their origin, former management and water source should be researched where possible, before making any decisions about their restoration. Drastic change should always be avoided. The Wychwood Project can help provide specialist advice.

CONCLUSION

This description of Wychwood's landscape features which can be maintained and enhanced is not comprehensive. We have not touched upon the ancient green lanes, parks and heathland, or more recent habitats such as railway embankments and former quarries, both of which exist within the area. Nevertheless, we have given simple guidelines which can be followed in much of Wychwood.

Until quite recently, many landscapes were cherished for their usefulness and beauty. Nowadays we appreciate additional qualities, for example in Wychwood signs of its history and evolution. We also know that landscapes provide habitats, not only for human beings but also

126

for the many other creatures and plants that occupy the world around us. If well managed, Wychwood can become a richer place for all its inhabitants, including its wildlife.

SOURCES OF ADVICE

- Wychwood Project
- Oxfordshire Woodland Project
- West Oxfordshire District Council
- Oxfordshire County Council
- FWAG (Farming and Wildlife Advisory Group)
- ESA (Upper Thames Tributaries Environmentally Sensitive Area) – Farming and Rural Conservation Agency
- Countryside Stewardship – Farming and Rural Conservation Agency
- Environment Agency
- Forestry Authority

SOURCES AND FURTHER READING

Atlantic Consultants, *West Oxfordshire Landscape Assessment*, 1998, West Oxfordshire District Council.

Broad, Ken, *Caring for Small Woods*, 1998, Earthscan Publications Ltd.

Fairbrother, Nan, *The Nature of Landscape Design*, 1974, Architectural Press.

FWAG publications: *Arable Farming; Farming for Biodiversity* (with BBONT, now BBOWT); *Farming and Field Margins;* and *The Good Hedge Guide* (with Bayer plc).

North Leigh Common

There were several areas of heath within the historic Forest. Ramsden Heath and Finstock Heath are still marked on the Ordnance Survey maps, but the largest area of heathland lay between North Leigh, Freeland and Eynsham, and the remnant survives today as North Leigh Common.

In these heathy places the underlying geology is overlain by glacial sands and gravels which support plants that thrive on acid soils, such as Yorkshire fog, velvet bent, wavy hair grass (all grasses), harebell, heath bedstraw and gorse. Heather was last recorded on North Leigh Common in 1976 and the open areas of the Common have been largely taken over by bracken which is very invasive.

Before the enclosures, which in this case mostly took place in the second half of the

NORTH LEIGH COMMON TODAY

eighteenth century, North Leigh Common and surrounding area were common grazing land. The largest area was Eynsham Heath, which covered the whole of modern Eynsham Park, and the land on both sides of Cuckoo Lane as far east as Freeland. Hanborough Heath ran east and north from the present Common as far as the steep side of the Evenlode valley. The Common itself also extended further north, into East End. The major part of North Leigh Common lay to the south west of North Leigh (hence 'Common Road'), while Hailey had a strip of heath adjoining to the west. There are numerous clues to the former heath in place names surviving today such as Moorland and Heath Holm Farms in New Yatt; and Blindwell Gorse and North Gorse in Eynsham Park – gorse being a typical plant of heathland.

The rights to graze animals and cut fuel on the heath were very important to the poor of the neighbourhood. As the more powerful in the locality attempted to enclose parts of the heath in the late seventeenth and early eighteenth centuries, in order to bring the land into more productive use, there were sometimes violent protests. The best known of these is the 'rabbit throwing' riot in 'Ensham Heath' in 1696 when a large crowd of people, including some from North Leigh, broke open some man-made rabbit warrens and threw the rabbits at Ursula Jourdan, wife of Thomas Jourdan who had recently built a house on the heath and may have tried to enclose land around it.

Despite protests, the move towards enclosure was unstoppable. North Leigh was one of the first parishes in the county to be enclosed, under private Act of Parliament passed in 1758. A map of Eynsham Heath of 1769 appears to show that by then Eynsham Park was already enclosed. Part of the south-western heath remained as common land until a second enclosure award in 1814, whilst the area

DAVIS'S MAP OF OXFORDSHIRE, 1797 (DETAIL). A DOTTED OUTLINE IS SUPERIMPOSED TO SHOW THE COMMON, SEPARATED FROM EYNSHAM HEATH BY A HEDGE. THE DARK AREA IS EYNSHAM HALL.

now known as the Common remained open.

From the time of enclosure until at least 1900 it is clear from old maps that the Common was an important source of sand and clay for brick making. Several brick kilns are shown nearby and clay pits and sand pits are shown on nineteenth-century maps. These pits are still evident today although they have become rather overgrown. The Common must also have been grazed until, perhaps, the First World War, since it is not until the 1920s that maps show the encroachment of trees onto this previously open ground.

The Common is managed by West Oxfordshire District Council. A management plan has recently been prepared which includes proposals to control the bracken, and to try to re-establish some areas of heather. It is possible that some heather seed still remains in the ground and may germinate if patches of bracken are cleared. Heather is being re-established in this way at a similar site at Nettlebed in South Oxfordshire. The acid grassland is also an unusual habitat in West Oxfordshire and the aim is to increase the area of this, again by controlling bracken.

Bracken is not only difficult and time consuming to control, but it also contributes to the character of the Common. It would not therefore be practical or visually desirable to eradicate it completely. The long-term aim is to reduce it by 50-75%, replacing it with heather or acid grassland species, depending on the success of the restoration and the resources available. There are several ways to control bracken. One is to cut it back to ground level, preferably three times a year in June, July and August, and to remove the litter. Alternatively a dedicated herbicide can be effective and less labour intensive.

Much of the Common is now covered by scrub and woodland, and this too needs management to improve its wildlife interest. The main proposals are to coppice the shrubby species such as hawthorn gradually on a ten-year rotation, to achieve a better age rank and thicker understorey. The dense blackthorn scrub is potentially valuable for the rare black hairstreak butterfly, which was last recorded on the Common in 1988, and the dense scrub generally provides feeding and relatively undisturbed nesting sites for birds. The proposal is to cut this scrub on a long rotation of perhaps 30 years, cutting one block every 5 years, with a mixture of coppicing and laying.

The overgrown sand and clay pits will be opened up by removing or coppicing about half the willows and other trees overhanging the numerous ponds, to help prevent the ponds drying out in summer.

The Council also intends to provide low-key interpretation boards, both to explain the management and highlight features of interest.

AMANDA HOPWOOD, *landscape architect, BHWB Environmental Design and Planning*

Three Wychwood Walks

ALAN SPICER

These three walks set out from Charlbury, which is in the centre of the Wychwood area and is served by bus and rail. They give a sample of the Wychwood landscape. Grid references are provided for specific points along the trails to enable walkers to locate their position on the Ordnance Survey maps of the area. Please keep to the footpaths.

These walks are in addition to the Wychwood Way, a 37-mile circular walk created by the Wychwood Project to celebrate the Millennium, which passes through Blenheim, Combe, North Leigh, Ramsden, Leafield, Ascott-under-Wychwood, Chadlington, Spelsbury, and Stonesfield.

WALK 1   CORNBURY PARK AND WYCHWOOD FOREST *13 km (8 miles)*

This walk passes through three distinct types of landscape: parkland, woodland and river valley, with panoramic views over the surrounding countryside. Part of the walk follows an ancient track through remnants of Wychwood Forest. This area is a nationally important nature reserve, so please stay on the path and keep dogs on leads along this stretch of the route. It is muddy in places so good footwear is advisable.

SP353195 **1** Starting at the station in Charlbury, cross over the river towards the town. Take the first turn to the right, leading past the church. An old story says that local deer poachers used to hide their venison in some of the graves. Turn right out of the churchyard and follow the road.

SP357190 **2** On the right there is a good view of Cornbury Park with a classic parkland mixture of grassland and trees, some very ancient.

A little further along, on the left, is a wall with large clipped yews through which can be glimpsed Lee Place, a house dating in part from the seventeenth century and named after the Lee family of Ditchley who owned it for a time in the eighteenth century. Its present owner is the Duke of Marlborough.

Turn right opposite the lodge gates to cross the railway and the River Evenlode.

SP355188 **3** The road enters Cornbury Park at North Lodge and leads to Cornbury House, but the public footpath turns left just before the gates to the Park through the painted door on the left. Cornbury originated

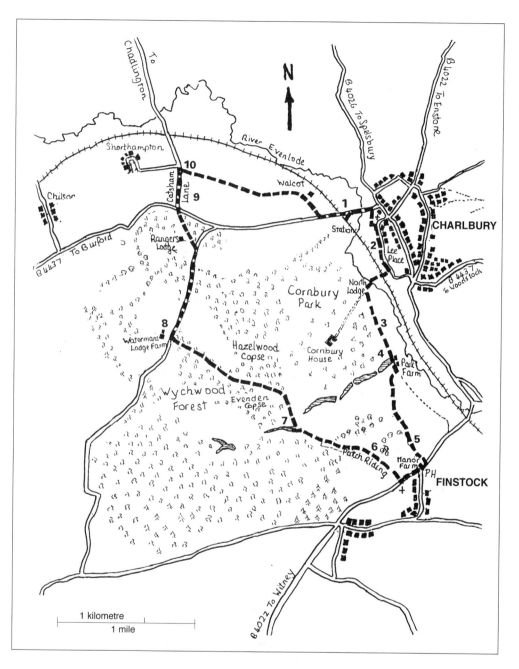

as a royal hunting lodge in Wychwood Forest and was normally granted to the Ranger of the Forest.

The path follows the tall deer fence along the side of the park, which has a typical landscape of large old pollarded trees, mostly oak with some horse chestnut.

SP358180   **4** As the path approaches Park Farm look out on the right for an igloo-shaped building in the park. This is an ice house, which stored ice collected in the winter for use throughout the summer. The trail passes along the dam forming the lowest of a series of seven artificial lakes, originally built as three fishponds in Wychwood.

Take a track to the right, opposite a group of cottages, leading between paddocks and continue along a broad grassy avenue.

SP358174   **5** Go straight over at a junction of tracks and then bear left along a narrower track, which further along is edged on the right with a small copse of hazel. The track bends and crosses a small steep valley, the sides of which have been left unploughed for many years. This provides cover for pheasants and also links several small pieces of woodland to the benefit of wildlife.

The track reaches a group of old farm buildings around a meadow. The tall three-storey house is Manor Farm dating back to 1660. Go through the gate and cross the lawn.

Climb over the stone stile and cross the road with great care as traffic is fast here. Turn right along the road-side verge. At the junction re-cross the road with care and continue along the verge, past a lay-by until a track turns off on the right.

SP358168   **6** The track is called Patch Riding and leads into the remnants of Wychwood Forest. Look for fossils in the remnants of old stone walls to the right. These are remains of shellfish preserved in marine deposits which formed the rock millions of years ago when this area was covered by a shallow sea.

The track descends and rises, passing another area of hazel coppice, this time interspersed with tall standard oaks. Follow the sign, through a gateway, and carry on downhill between the banks which often have primroses in spring and foxgloves in summer.

The clean, spring-fed lake in the valley bottom is of national importance, supporting a rich variety of aquatic wildlife.

SP348172   **7** The trail then bears right and climbs uphill, then emerges on an open grassy area with a wall beyond, which is the boundary of Cornbury Park. Follow the signs, leaving the track and crossing the grass taking the second left to walk up a broad ride.

Continue straight on along this track which can become quite muddy. On each side there are banks marking the different copses in the Forest. Along this path you will see several typical woodland plants including early purple orchids, with their blotchy leaves growing early in the spring. Take care not to trample plants growing on the path.

SP332181   **8** The path now reaches the road. Climb over the stile and turn right, continuing along the road for about 2 km (about 1mile). To the left is an open area with a house and farm buildings. This is Ranger's Lodge, where there has been a large clearing for several hundred years, part of which was a sheep walk where flocks belonging to Shorthampton villagers had grazing rights.

At the road junction take the road signed Chadlington.

Just before the next junction there is an opportunity to pause and look at the view, much of which covers the second half of the Saltway North Walk (Walk 2). From right to left, on the skyline the line of trees is Shilcott Wood, with the hamlet of Taston just visible behind the tower of Spelsbury church; the square of woodland in the valley is Dean Grove. An uncultivated rectangular patch on the hillside across the valley further to the left is Knollbury Camp, thought to date from the Iron Age.

SP333195   **9** Cross the road into Catsham Lane, which continues straight on downhill. The verges here are worth looking at, as they contain a good variety of limestone grassland plants. The verge by the layby on the left is a county nature reserve.

SP334200   **10** Continue downhill until a track leads off to the right, marked Oxfordshire Way. A short diversion to Shorthampton can be taken here by carrying on a little further and taking the lane to the left. The Norman church has remains of medieval wall paintings.

SP346198   **11** The Oxfordshire Way is followed back to Charlbury. The path dips down to a hedge, which forms part of the parish boundary between Chilson and Charlbury.

SP349194   **12** When the track meets the road, turn left towards Charlbury. As you cross the railway bridge, there is a good view of the little station which was designed by Isambard Kingdom Brunel and is now a listed building. The walk ends at the station.

WALKS
2 & 3   THE SALTWAY NORTH AND SOUTH

ACCESS ROUTES FROM CHARLBURY TO THE SALTWAY FOR WALKS 2 AND 3

An interesting old track leads from the centre of Charlbury to the Saltway where either the North or South Saltway trails (Walks 2 and 3) can be taken. There are two further ways of reaching the Saltway, outlined at the end of this section. All three can be used to vary the distance of the Saltway walks.

SP358197   **1** The walk starts at the Spendlove car park in the centre of Charlbury. Take the road opposite the entrance, following the right-hand side of the Playing Close, which was a recreation ground as early as 1447 and continued to be used for bull baiting and fairs up to the nineteenth century.

Continue to the bottom of the hill and take the footpath on the left which follows a stream, lined with pollarded willows, to the main road. Cross the road and take the footpath opposite alongside a house called Blenheim Farmhouse and follow it through a narrow area known as Sandford Slade. The name 'slade' refers to a muddy or waterlogged area and a spring rises in this small valley where the surface geology changes from limestone to clay.

SP365195　**2**　The path continues climbing up the slope through two small fields, the second of which is the first community nature reserve set up by BBONT: the Berks, Bucks and Oxon Naturalists' Trust (now called BBO Wildlife Trust). The reserve is run by and for the local community and is an area of semi-improved limestone grassland where so far over fifty types of grassland plants have been recorded.

SP366195　**3**　The trail continues over a stile beside spreading field maple trees, the only native British maple, more often seen as a hedge species. The path leads along the edge of a field but soon becomes enclosed on both sides. This field was planted as a community woodland to celebrate the completion of a century of public service by the Oxfordshire County Council in 1989. It is part of the Wychwood Project, which encourages such habitat restoration schemes.

The track is here called the Woodstock Way. Before the days of the turnpike road which now links Charlbury and Woodstock, this was the lane which led to the Saltway, the ancient track between Chipping Norton and Stonesfield.

SP369197　**4**　The trail reaches a junction with another path from the left, but carries straight on. In the near distance to the left is a disused quarry, excavated during the last thirty years, part of which is a geological Site of Special Scientific Interest (SSSI). It shows the succession in rock formation as layers of limestone were deposited during the Jurassic period about 164 to 170 million years ago.

SP375198　**5**　As the path continues, evidence of the earlier proximity of woodland is shown in the adjacent field names. To the right lies Woodfield and Stump Ground, whilst, as the path bears left, the old use of the path is shown in Mile Oak Piece, where an oak marked a mile from Charlbury.

SP381200　**6**　Woodstock Way meets the Saltway at Dustfield Farm, which is on the site of a very early clearing in the woodland, known as *Dustlefeld* in 1300. Another name for the Saltway is Mereway, from the Old English *(ge)maere* meaning boundary, which demonstrates the antiquity of the track.

Turn left to follow Walk 2, Saltway North, and right for Walk 3, Saltway South.

SECOND ACCESS TO WALKS 2 AND 3

Turn left on the road up the hill from the Spendlove car park, past the recreation ground to the crossroads. Turn right here, pass the youth hostel, and then immediately turn left along Ditchley Road. On the way there are several bends in the road. After the third bend the road follows Grim's Ditch for a while. The road leads to the Saltway, joining it at the lodge gates to Ditchley Estate.

THIRD ACCESS TO WALK 2 AND 3

Again turn left from the Spendlove car park, up the hill. At the crossroads keep straight on for a short distance before taking a path slightly to the right called Hundley Way. Follow this path until it meets the Saltway at SP377210.

WALK 2   SALTWAY NORTH *13 km (8 miles)*

Having reached the Saltway via one of the three access routes described, the walk follows this ancient drove track. It descends into the Evenlode valley through Taston and Spelsbury, leading back to Charlbury through ancient woodland and a series of old fields and lanes.

SP381201   **1** Turn left at Dustfield Farm from Woodstock Way. The flora of the Saltway is obviously much richer than that of the field path you have just walked. See how many different flowers you can find, but don't pick them!

SP380206   **2** A road from Charlbury crosses the trail and enters the Ditchley Estate. (This is the second access point; turn left here onto the trail.) Ditchley has a long history, beginning with a Roman villa which was the centre of an estate of a thousand acres and was used into the fifth century. The name Ditchley dates from Saxon times and means 'the clearing (*leah*) by the ditch', referring to Grim's Ditch, an Iron Age linear earthwork.

SP379208   **3** Along this stretch of the Saltway, look out for plant species which prefer a lime-rich soil such as cowslip, scabious and St John's wort. Hundley Way, the third access track, joins the Saltway near here.

SP374214   **4** Opposite a house called Norman's Grove, over the stone wall, remains of a pond are still apparent with some old pollarded willows growing alongside. The hedges are covered with black bryony, with shiny arrow-shaped leaves. The bright yellow and red fruit is poisonous to humans but is eaten by birds after it has been frosted during the winter. Shilcott Wood on the right is a remnant of ancient woodland.

SP370217   **5** Keep to the right as the track forks. As it emerges from the edge of Shilcott Wood, the trail descends a gentle slope. Keep to the central path, as the track is bordered by trenches which are obscured by scrub.

SP367221   **6** The track crosses the Charlbury-Enstone road and continues with good views on the left-hand side across to the present-day Wychwood Forest to the south and to the Burford-Stow ridge on the skyline to the west.

After crossing the Taston-Enstone road, the ground becomes rather sticky as the soil is clay. A nearby field is called Brickground and the long disused small quarries in this vicinity, also remembered in the field name of Second Slat Pits, indicate that in the past this area must have been quite an industrial site.

SP357232   **7** After about 1 km (half a mile) take the footpath to the sharp left, bearing diagonally left to reach a farm track. Bear right and after about 500 yards cross a stile.

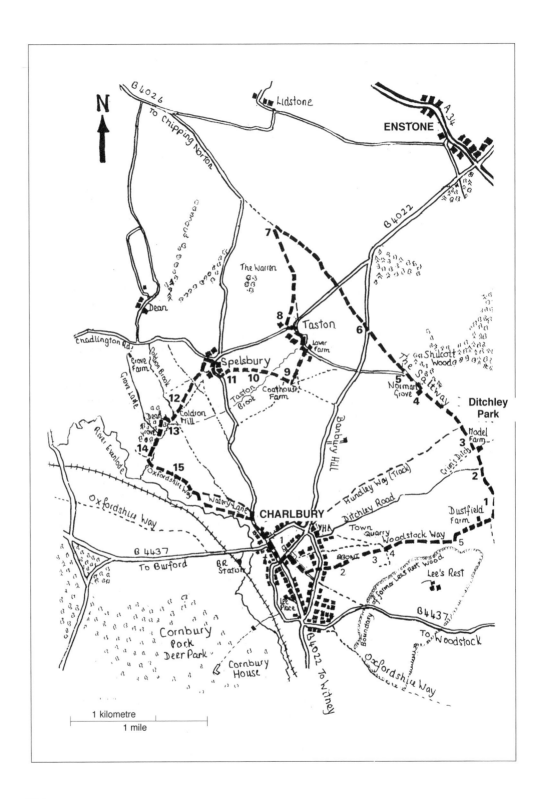

SP359222   **8** Turn right down the road, to reach a junction at the entrance to the village of Taston. Follow the road through the village. Taston gets its name from an ancient standing stone, the Thor Stone, still in place in a cottage hedge near the remains of the old village cross.

After a left-hand bend in the road, past Lower Farm, take the track to the right and walk uphill past several houses to Coathouse Farm which stands alone in the fields.

SP359215   **9** Turn right here, following the parish boundary hedge. The path here is very different from the grassy track of the Saltway. This little valley is below the spring line and the ground is much damper as the soil is clay rather than limestone. The grass has been taken over by tall, tussocky species which crowd out most of the flowering plants.

The path continues to a marshy area (where care or good footwear is necessary!) which has some interesting plants not often seen in the surrounding well-drained agricultural land. Continue across stepping stones over Taston Brook. The steep banks provide a habitat for moisture- and sun-loving plants, a contrast to the shady damp area just walked through. Depending on the season, ragged robin, meadow sweet, water forget-me-not and marsh marigold can be seen.

The trail crosses diagonally left over the next field, an example of ridge-and-furrow which has remained undisturbed by ploughs since the Middle Ages.

SP355217   **10** Looking back across the small valley to the south-east is the site of the deserted medieval village of Cote, whose presence is remembered in Coathouse Farm as well as several field names – Cote Coppice, Coate Grounds and Hovel Ground.

SP350217   **11** The trail now reaches Spelsbury. Turn left and cross the road with care, then right along the road, past the old water fountain. Note the commemorative plaque. The nearby church is worth a detour as it contains memorials to many of the owners of the manor over the centuries. Take the Chadlington road, and turn left after about ten metres down an unmade road, which leads across the fields at the back of the churchyard.

SP345211   **12** The track leads to Coldron Mill, which was a working mill for at least a thousand years. When it fell into disuse after the First World War, the grinding gear was taken to the London Science Museum, but was destroyed in bombing in the Second World War.

SP344210   **13** Keeping the wet area and the row of sloes trees to the left, the trail crosses a stile and small stream, passing through a small meadow. One plant of interest is lady's mantle with pleated leaves and green-yellow flowers.

The path leads straight on through a gate into a wood, where it turns left. This is Dean Grove, part of an area of woodland recorded in the Domesday Book. It is an area of mostly hazel coppice with a rich woodland flora, flowering in the spring. The ground can be wet.

SP343206   **14** The trail leaves the wood and crosses a grassy field to a gate, and then diagonally left across the next field to a wooden footbridge across Coldron Brook, the parish boundary at this point. Here the trail meets the Oxfordshire Way.

SP344205   **15** The trail and the Oxfordshire Way follow the same route back to Charlbury, so look for the waymarks. The path skirts a patch of rough ground containing gorse with the appropriate field-name of Low Furze. This is probably a remnant of part of the old common. The path then runs along the edge of woodland.

The trail turns right on reaching Water Lane which tends to live up to its name, so an alternative route leaves the lane by a stile on the left after a short distance and continues ahead across three fields. The path joins the Charlbury-Spelsbury road, with Charlbury to the right. The Spendlove car park is found by taking the second turning on the left in the town, while the station is sign-posted to the right.

WALK 3   **SALTWAY SOUTH**   *10 km (6 miles)*

This walk is based on the southern portion of the Saltway, which can be reached by any of the three access routes described earlier. The trail leads to Stonesfield, a village which dates back to Roman times and has a recent industrial interest. The return to Charlbury is via part of the Oxfordshire Way which follows the old boundary of Lee's Rest Wood.

SP383197   **1** Turn south at any of the access points (that is, Dustfield Farm, Ditchley Gate or Hundley Way). The most interesting part of the Saltway soon becomes apparent. It widens out to a maximum of about 25 metres and contains a rich and varied flora.

SP388192   **2** Here the Saltway meets a more recent road, the turnpike of 1800 between Charlbury and Woodstock, which was based on one of the tracks through Lee's Rest Wood. Cross the road and follow the path along the hedge.

SP390189   **3** The hedge for part of its length forms a parish boundary between Fawler and Spelsbury. It follows a sinuous curve, which often indicates a boundary hedge, and also contains a high number of species. The path passes through a gate near Newbarn Farm, which is shown on a map of 1797. Sheer's Copse, which lies behind the farm, is a remnant of Wychwood Forest, but is now a mixture of broad-leaved deciduous species and conifers.

SP393186   **4** Going through two small fields, the trail continues along a track with an unspoilt verge and hedge on the right, whilst on the left you are likely to see intensively cultivated cereal crops. The track becomes muddy as it dips into the head of a small valley.

SP395182   **5** Turning right, the trail leads onto Stonesfield Riding, an old lane, which from its name originally went through woodland. The field on the right is known Gerner's Sart, 'sart' being a corruption of assart, meaning clearing of woodland. A perambulation of Wychwood dated

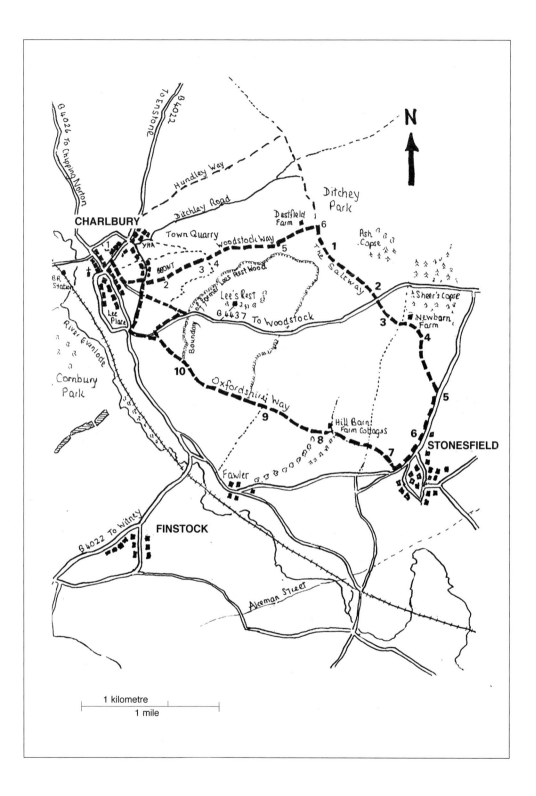

1298 records Gerner's Wood here and it possible that this field dates from about this time.

SP391173   6   Keep going straight on through the village, following signpost to Charlbury, and look out for the village tap on the left about halfway down the hill. There are pubs and shops in Stonesfield. Stonesfield was famous for its production of slates until the late nineteen century.

At the bottom of the hill, turn right up a stony track where the trail meets the Oxfordshire Way. Look back for a good view of Stonesfield – the old village is a typical 'industrial' collection of closely-packed cottages, compared to the later and modern arrangement with gardens.

SP384177   7   The trail leads straight on, through large arable fields, following the route of a well defined track between Charlbury and Stonesfield shown on the map of 1797 and defined as a public road on the Charlbury Tithe Award Map of 1847.

SP382177   8   The path bears left through a gate and starts to descend into a small valley near Hill Barn Farm Cottages.

SP374181   9   After about 1km (0.5 mile) a path to the left leads to Fawler, formerly a hamlet in Charlbury parish, where Roman remains were found in the nineteenth century.

The Oxfordshire Way continues straight on. The track becomes hedged on both sides and within a short distance follows, on the right, the southern edge of the site of Lee's Rest Wood, part of Wychwood Forest.

SP364186   10 Gaps in the hedge to the left provide a wide view across to Cornbury Park and the remaining Wychwood Forest, and also to Leafield on the skyline with its church steeple and clump of trees standing on top of a Bronze Age round barrow.

The trail meets the B4437 on the outskirts of Charlbury. The Spendlove car park can be reached by turning left onto the road and then taking the right turn at Five-ways junction. Follow this road for about 400 metres until the footpath opposite Blenheim Farmhouse is reached and retrace your steps to the car park.

Fuller accounts of these and other walks in the Wychwood area are contained in the Oxfordshire Country Walks series, Volume1, *Evenlode and Wychwood* and Volume 5, *Glyme Valley*, available from Charlbury railway station, and from local visitor information centres, shops and libraries.

Gazetteer

Each entry contains at least some of the following information, in this order:

location; derivation of name; items of historical interest; architectural significance; local services; landscape features; important wildlife habitats in that particular parish; walks.

Almost without exception each settlement is built mostly of local Cotswold stone. Regrettably several of the villages nowadays have no local services, not even a public house or shop. Some of the churches are locked up at least during the week. The information about local services was collected in summer 1999, and may change. The following abbreviations are used: PH for public house, and PO for post office.

ASCOTT-UNDER-WYCHWOOD

On the river Evenlode 2 km (1.5 miles) downstream from Shipton-under-Wychwood. From the Old English *Estcote*. The modern village was originally two settlements, Ascott d'Oyley after the family of Wido de Oileio who accompanied William the Conqueror, and to the west Ascott Earl, possibly from the Earls of Gloucester who held part of Ascott. Remains of a motte and bailey castle in each. In 1873 the Ascott martyrs, local women, were imprisoned for protesting against agricultural strike-breakers on Crown Farm. Holy Trinity Church, partly Norman, is set in a large churchyard with avenue of limes. Railway station, with very few stopping trains into and out of Oxford. Swan PH. The landscape is a mix of grass and arable fields, smaller to the N. Priest Grove and Boynal Copse, currently a conifer plantation, S of the parish were originally part of Wychwood. Along the railway line important wildlife habitats of limestone grassland and scrub support characteristic species, e.g. wild liquorice and pale toadflax. A private nature reserve created at Manor Farm. Footpaths up and down the Evenlode, and SE to Leafield. On the Wychwood Way.

ASTHALL

On the River Windrush 4 km (3 miles) downstream from Burford amongst meadows. In 1086, *Esthale*. Originally a small Romano-British settlement on Akeman Street. St Nicholas Church, transitional Norman, with pretty late Victorian wall paintings in the chancel. The present Manor House, built c.1620 and enlarged 1916, was the home of Lord Redesdale and the Mitford Family. The Maytime Inn, restaurant and accommodation. A hilly parish falling down to the Windrush, with many small- to medium-sized arable and grass fields with prominent, intact hedgerows and stone walls. Wet grassland and marsh on the river plain, which floods in winter, are attractive to wildfowl. Plant species include early marsh orchid. On the drier slopes of the valley are areas of limestone grassland. Walks upstream towards Swinbrook and Burford, downstream to Minster Lovell.

ASTHALL LEIGH

Small hamlet 2 km (1.5 miles) NE of Asthall, known before the 19th century as 'Astally'. Means 'clearing in Asthall's wood', which was a long tongue of woodland running south from Field Assarts towards Old Minster. On the fringe of the Forest until the 19th-century clearances, Asthall Leigh itself was already enclosed in small parcels of clearings by the time of the 1812 Enclosure Award map. Small 19th-century chapel, now deconsecrated. Large mixed plantation remains N of the parish at Stockley Copse, and several smaller deciduous copses to the S.

BABLOCK HYTHE

On the Thames, 2 km (1.5 miles) SE of Stanton Harcourt. From the Old English meaning 'Babba's Landing Place'. In the Middle Ages, a ferry on the perimeter of the Forest area and last used as a vehicle ferry in 1970s. Nowadays The Ferryman Inn and caravan site on the Thames Path.

BARNARD GATE

5 km (3 miles) E of Witney, a hamlet on a loop of the old A40. The lost medieval village of Tilgarsley, which died out during the Black Death, lay nearby. Literally 'Tilgar's clearing'. The old village fields lie S of Eynsham Hall, and although there is no archaeological evidence, the village itself may have been located near modern day Bowles Farm. The Boot Inn, specialising in food.

BRUERN

Near the River Evenlode, 3 km (2 miles) NE of Shipton-under-Wychwood. From the Old French, meaning Heath. Nothing remains of the Cistercian abbey founded in 1137 except the site of its fish pond, still frequented by herons. The present house was built in 1720, simple local Baroque. A well-wooded landscape. Milton Heath lay S of Bruern Wood until its enclosure in 19th century. Some of woods ancient and others originally parkland support a range of woodland ground flora and are also excellent bird habitats. W of the parish are ancient woodlands at Tangley. Woodland walks at Berks Bucks and Oxfordshire Wildlife Trust's reserve at Foxholes, and at Bruern Wood (with permit).

BURFORD

10 km (7 miles) W of Witney at crossing of A40 and A361. One of the best-known Cotswold towns, just south of the Windrush, and hence just outside the Norman royal Forest. Essentially still a small medieval town, with a range of 14th- to 16th-century houses and numerous inns remaining. The Church of St John the Baptist is a large and complicated building, with a Norman core and surrounding chapels, which was remodelled in the 15th century. A memorial to Henry VIII's surgeon Edmund Harman interestingly includes American Indians. The churchyard was the scene of England's Tiananmen Square – in 1649 Cromwell had three mutinous Levellers shot and buried there. As well as the High Street, Witney Street and Sheep Street contain many handsome houses and inns. Golf course. E and W of the town centre are small blocks of woodland. The wet grasslands and marsh of the river valley provide particularly notable bird habitats. For more information contact the Tourist Information Office, The Brewery, Sheep Street, tel. 01993 823558.

CHADLINGTON

5 km (3.5 miles) S of Chipping Norton, a long village (divided into five 'ends', some of which are almost separate hamlets) which overlooks the broad Evenlode valley towards the remnants of Wychwood. From the Old English, *Ceadala's hill* (or possibly after St Chad). *Cedelintone* in Domesday book. There is a mysterious earthwork, Knollbury, to the NE. Saxon graves found S of the village near Catsham bridge. St Nicholas Church was originally Norman, with many subsequent alterations and additions, including gargoyles and a Green Man. The Tite Inn with restaurant. Butcher, grocer and PO stores. Large arable fields above the village. Several streams flow through the parish to join the river Evenlode below. There has been some hedgerow loss. Small blocks of woodland lie to the S of the village, with some new tree planting above the village. Upper Court Farm currently participates in the Countryside Stewardship scheme, as the mellow colours of its fields show, and there are permissive walks around these fields. Wild grape hyacinths grow on the old allotment site near Westend. Walks along the river to Ascott or

Charlbury, and up a green lane north towards Chipping Norton. On the Wychwood Way.

CHARLBURY

On the Evenlode, 9 km (6 miles) SE of Chipping Norton. From the Old English, *Ceorls' burgh*, or 'freemen's fortified place'. In 1094 Charlbury belonged to Eynsham Abbey. In 1256 it became a market town and wide Church Street still feels like a market place leading down to the parish church of St Mary. This has Norman origins but has been heavily remodelled, most recently in the early 1990s – unusually the congregation now face west. Charlbury also has Methodist, Baptist and Roman Catholic churches and a Friends' Meeting House, sympathetically extended in 1991. Lee Place, traditionally the former Dower House of Ditchley and now the summer home of the Duke of Marlborough, is a perfect small park and house (not open to the public). Playing Close is a pretty small town green. Previously a centre of gloving, the last manufacturer of gloves closed in Charlbury in 1960s. Several shops, including pharmacy, grocery, butcher, bookshop, PO and newsagent. Youth Hostel, Coffee house, The Bell Hotel and restaurant, The Bull PH and restaurant, The Rose & Crown and the Farmers Arms PHs both with pub food. Holiday accommodation, camping and caravan site at Banbury Hill Farm. Also a camp site on the Spelsbury road. Good train services to Oxford, London and W towards Worcester. Charlbury is a hilly parish dropping to the river. Many hedgerows still exist, some ancient, together with several green lanes and small woodlands. Ancient hedgerows to the E of the town mark the boundary of Lee's Rest Wood, a significant former area of Forest woodland, which in the Middle Ages was known as Abbey Wood and belonged to Eynsham Abbey. Cornbury deer park and a large remnant of Wychwood are nearby. Important wildlife habitats include the River Evenlode, limestone grassland throughout the parish, some scrubby areas which provide good bird habitats, marshy patches to the NW of the parish and a quarry of geological interest. As well as Centenary Community wood, there are local nature reserves at Wigwell Valley and Blenheim Farm. There are good local walks up the Evenlode to Chadlington, E towards Ditchley, and SE to Stonesfield. The Oxfordshire Way runs through the town.

CHILSON

A hamlet, S of the River Evenlode between Charlbury and Ascott-under-Wychwood. From the Old English, meaning 'Young nobleman's dwelling'. Chilson, consisting of a few substantial farm houses and cottages, stands to the north of the remnant of Wychwood. The village is surrounded by medium-sized fields, many with low but intact hedgerows. Knighton's Copse, to the SW, is an ancient woodland site but is now mainly plantation.

CHIPPING NORTON

High on the Cotswolds, an unspoilt market town just to the north of Wychwood. There are remains of a motte and bailey castle near the Church of St Mary. This church was rebuilt in 1485 and has a fine lofty interior. Towards the town centre from the church is a row of almshouses, 1640. The Guildhall in Middle Row is 16th century. E of the Market Place, many houses were refronted handsomely in the 18th century. There are a number of interesting 19th-century buildings, including the neo-classical Town Hall of 1842 in the Tuscan style, massive Bliss Tweed Mill just west of the town, 1872, and several unusual 'mixed Renaissance' buildings, for example the Co-op of 1890. The town has its own theatre, tel. 01608 642350. Golf course. Market day Wednesday. Outside the town, especially to S, woodland is scarce and many of the arable fields have low gappy hedgerows. Key wildlife habitats are limestone grassland and woodland in the steep tree-lined valley to the W of the town, and around the source of the River Glyme to the E. For further information about Chipping Norton, contact the Tourist Information office at the Guildhall, tel. 01608 644379.

CHURCH HANBOROUGH

2 km (1 mile) S of Long Hanborough, off A4095. From the Old English, 'Hane's Hill'. A compact village, with church of St Peter and St Paul at its centre. Some Norman carving in the tympanum of the N doorway, but mostly Perpendicular. Elegant spire and interior. Hand and Shears PH, food and drink. The village is set in gently undulating countryside just above the Evenlode. Surrounding fields bounded by tree-lined hedges. Nearby Pinsley Wood is an ancient remnant of Wychwood.

CHURCHILL

5 km (3 miles) SW of Chipping Norton. Literally 'hill hill'. The original medieval church lies to the NW of the village. Its replacement, All Saints, was built in 1826. A local landmark, its tower is a reduced version of the tower of Magdalen College, Oxford, and its hammerbeam roof is copied from Christ Church, Oxford. Interesting memorials in the village, including a monolith to William Smith, a founder of modern geology. The Forge Guest House. This is a hilly parish on the fringes of the Forest. Some small to medium fields still

survive near the village, especially in the Sars Brook valley to E, the Norman Forest boundary in this area. Elsewhere fields are large and mostly arable, with hedgerows. Important wildlife habitats include limestone grassland to the W of the parish, and ancient woodland at Sarsgrove Wood. Walks up Sars Brook valley, and N of village along Bestbury Lane and towards Churchill Grounds Farm. The d'Arcy Dalton way passes through the village.

COMBE

Just N of the River Evenlode, 5 km (3 miles) west of Woodstock. From the Celtic *cumb*, meaning 'at the valley'. The parish dips steeply S to the river. Some suggest the village moved up from the valley to its present site in the Middle Ages. St Laurence Church was rebuilt by Eynsham Abbey in 1395 and has been little altered, broad and simple with some interesting wall paintings. There is a village green, where Combe Feast is held on the second Sunday in August, with a fair on Monday and Tuesday following. The Cock Inn, with bar meals. Combe Stores. Combe Mill, 1 mile SE towards Long Hanborough, is Blenheim's saw mill. Its 19th-century beam steam engine runs from time to time in the summer as a public display. Very few trains to and from Oxford stop at Combe Station, near the mill. Woodland is a dominant feature of the local landscape, including Notoaks Wood W of the village and copses in the Evenlode valley. Limestone grassland and scrub, especially near the railway and to W of the parish, contain characteristic species such as clustered bellflower, thyme, cowslip and marjoram, and support populations of small blue butterfly and marbled white butterfly. Access to remnants of ancient wood pasture in the W of Blenheim Park via Combe Gate. On the Wychwood Way.

CORNBURY

Cornbury House is 1.5 km (1 mile) SW of Charlbury. The home of Lord Rotherwick, this estate evolved from the remnants of Wychwood Forest, with the ancient deer park at its centre. Originally a royal hunting lodge, the present house was built in a number of phases, from the sixteenth century until 1906. The E, or Clarendon, wing was built in the 1660s. Although the grounds are not regularly open to the public, Cornbury hosts a number of events which provide an opportunity to experience this ancient house and landscape. The woodlands, many still recognisable as distinct copses, remained as royal Forest until 1850s when they were transferred to Lord Churchill in lieu of his rights as Keeper of the Forest. Ranger's Lodge to the N was the home of the manager of the former royal woodlands while Waterman's

Lodge and High Lodge to the W housed forest keepers. Most of the parish is a key wildlife area, dominated by ancient broadleaved woodlands. Set within are areas of limestone grassland and old marl lakes. All these habitats have a very diverse flora and fauna, including national and county rarities. A footpath traverses the Forest from Finstock towards Chilson and another follows the NE side of the deer park, linking Finstock and Charlbury.

CRAWLEY

On the Windrush, 2 km (1.5 miles) NW of Witney. From the Old English, meaning 'crow wood'. There have been nearby mills on the Windrush for centuries. The Lamb Inn and restaurant, and The Crawley Inn, a drinkers' PH with occasional banquets. A hilly parish rising N from the river, on the fringe of Wychwood. There has been hedgerow loss to the N of the parish, but in the valley fields are smaller and surrounded by tall, prominent hedgerows. Marshy grassland bordering the Windrush, important for birds, and small ancient semi-natural woodland to the N of the parish are key wildlife habitats. Ancient trackways lie to the N of the parish, bordering the former woodlands and grasslands of Witney chase, hunting grounds of the Bishop of Winchester. Riverside walks up to Minster Lovell and into Witney.

DEAN

A completely unspoilt hamlet 1.5 km (1 mile) N of the River Evenlode, between Chadlington and Spelsbury. A classic small Queen Anne manor house. S of the village is Dean Common, the Wychwood Project's first community wood, which contains a variety of habitats. The Wychwood Way passes this hamlet.

DITCHLEY

4 km (3 miles) E of Charlbury, Ditchley Park is situated on the ancient earthwork of Grim's Ditch. Henry of Ditchley lived here in 13th century. The original house built by Sir Henry Lee, Forest Ranger of Woodstock to Elizabeth I, preceded the present house which was designed by James Gibbs in 1720. The park surrounding this house was naturalised with sweeping lawns in the 1760s, extended by Loudon in 1807 and redesigned by Sir Geoffrey Jellicoe in 1932. The estate is well wooded as a result of the Wills family's endeavours since World War II, some of the woodland retaining flora representative of the ancient Forest woodlands. Now the Ditchley Foundation occupies the house and park, which are not open to the public, but there are some public footpaths through the park and estate.

EAST END

A small linear hamlet 1.5 km (1 mile) NE of North Leigh. Remains of a large Roman villa, which faced SE overlooking the Evenlode flood plain (not currently open to the public). Leather Bottel guest house. Several footpaths meander down to the Evenlode valley. On the Wychwood Way.

ENSTONE

6 km (4 miles) SE of Chipping Norton on A44. From the Old English 'Enna's stone'. Half a mile S is the Hoar Stone, the remains of a prehistoric tomb. Some claim Enstone is England's largest parish. Previously on a busy road, Enstone is nowadays much quieter since the extension of the M40. St Kenelm's Church, to the E at Church Enstone, was built in stages on the site of a Saxon church from 1180 until 1546 when its substantial tower was completed. A barn, built by Winchcombe Abbey, to which Enstone belonged, stands nearby. Cleveley is an ancient hamlet 1 mile to SE. Fulwell, at the entrance to Ditchley, lies to the S. The Crown Inn PH with fresh food and rooms, and The Harrow Inn with pub food. PO and Stores. Surrounded by small to medium sized fields, with some well-maintained and some gappy hedgerows and walls. The parish supports a wide range of habitats, including semi-natural woodland, marsh, reedbeds, wetland, acidic grassland on drier slopes and limestone grassland and scrub. Nearby Heythrop Park also has a wide range of habitats, important for birds. Footpaths up the valley towards Heythrop, and down the valley towards Radford Bridge and Kiddington.

EVENLODE

This river runs SE through the middle of Wychwood, rising near Moreton-in-Marsh and joining the Thames just E of Eynsham. Previously known as the River Bladon. Good walks from Charlbury on the Oxfordshire Way right up to Kingham. The best views of this wide valley are from the brow of the hills, approaching Shipton-under-Wychwood from Swinbrook or Burford. The river and its margins are important habitats for birds such as swans, herons and kingfishers.

EYNSHAM

S of the A40, 7 km (5 miles) W of North Oxford, Eynsham straddled the old London to Gloucester coach road until the Oxford Northern by-pass was built between the wars. From the Old English, 'Aegan's home'. An early Saxon village has been excavated 1 mile NE of the town. A rich

Benedictine abbey, owning land throughout Oxfordshire including in Wychwood, existed W of the present Church of St Leonard, which was built between late 1200s and 1450. Contains elegant perpendicular work. The toll bridge SE of the town replaced a ford which existed until George III's reign. Nowadays modern developments surround the old centre of Eynsham, which remains mostly unspoilt with streets of stone cottages leading off the small Market Square. Eynsham has several PHs, restaurants and shops. The parish's larger hedgerows lie predominantly N of the A40, well away from the town. Walks along the Thames path, including to Oxford.

FAWLER

A hamlet on the River Evenlode 3 km (2 miles) SE of Charlbury. From Old English *fauflor*, meaning 'coloured floor', which may refer to the tesselated pavements of a Roman villa at Fawler (rediscovered in the 19th century when the railway was built). Old iron workings lie between the hamlet and Fawler mill. A dry, steep-sided wooded valley, known locally as Reed Hill, lies to E of the village. Reed Hill contains limestone grassland, woodland and scrub and is a valuable habitat for butterflies. Walks NE to the Oxfordshire Way between Charlbury and Stonesfield, and across the river towards Finstock, or through Topples Wood to Wilcote.

FIFIELD

7 km (5 miles) N of Burford and E of A424. 'Five Hides' in 1086. Fifield is a compact village, with several substantial houses. St John the Baptist Church, humble with an unusual octagonal tower with small spire. Merry Mouth Inn, with accommodation and food, on the main road. A hilly parish, straddling the watershed between the Evenlode and the Windrush. To the E of the village, large pastures with prominent hedgerows slope down towards the river Evenlode. Elsewhere mainly arable fields are surrounded by low, sometimes gappy hedges. Key wildlife habitats, extensive woodland and riverside marsh, are found to the NE of the parish. On foot Fifield is best approached from Herberts Heath near Bruern.

FINSTOCK

4 km (2.5 miles) S of Charlbury. Literally, 'place of the woodpecker'. Holy Trinity Church is Victorian, with an Edwardian chancel. Village Stores and PO. The Crown PH and Plough Inn with food and accommodation. Very few trains stop at Finstock station, in the valley towards Charlbury. A small hilly parish, which faces SE over the Evenlode

valley. The village is surrounded by small to medium sized fields, a mixture of grass and arable, with prominent hedgerows. Topples Wood, in the SE corner of the parish, is c.600 years old and is predominantly oak and ash, with a rich understorey of hawthorn, hazel and field maple and a ground flora including primrose and yellow archangel. SE of the village lie areas of limestone grassland. Public footpath into Wychwood Forest from opposite the church; and from lower down Charlbury Road. A walk leads NE along the edge of Cornbury deer park. Walks also towards Wilcote and Ramsden.

FORDWELLS

3 km (2 miles) N of Minster Lovell. Literally 'the spring by the ford'. The spring remains. In the Forest woodlands until the nineteenth-century clearances, when the hamlet was built and populated by local families who worked the newly cleared land. The first child was born here in 1860, and the 1861 census included 3 sawyers, a wheelwright and a carpenter all from the Bicester area in lodgings with a local agricultural labourer and his wife. Three of the four approaches to the hamlet are still wooded, with substantial woodlands W towards Swinbrook. There has been new planting in the valley towards Langley.

FREELAND

3 km (2 miles) N of Eynsham. Possibly carved by squatters out of heath on the edges of Eynsham, Freeland has grown subsequently and became a separate parish in 1869. St Mary's, a handsome High Victorian church by J. L. Pearson who also designed the parsonage and old school. Oxfordshire Yeoman PH, food and grills. Shepherds Hall Inn with food and accommodation, so-called from its location on a drove road (nowadays the A 4095). The gently undulating landscape is situated where Oxford clays meet oolitic limestone. Small to medium sized fields are surrounded by mainly intact hedgerows. Deciduous woodland lies SW of the village. Around Freeland House woodland, grassland and a lake provide rich habitats for birds and a wide flora. Walks S towards Vincent's Wood and E to Church Hanborough.

FULBROOK

1 km (0.5 mile) NE of Burford. Takes its name from 'foul' or 'dirty' brook, that flows S towards the Windrush. St James a fine Norman Church. One or two substantial houses in this long village. Masons Arms and the Carpenters Arms, both with food. Elm House private hotel. A hilly parish dropping to the Windrush valley. Originally on the edge of the Forest. Nowadays woodland is reduced to small blocks of

deciduous woodland N of the village. Important habitats include species-rich limestone grasslands which support a number of butterfly species.

GLYME

The river which lies along the eastern boundary of medieval Wychwood. From the Celtic, meaning 'bright river'. Rising near Chipping Norton, the Glyme joins the Evenlode just S of Blenheim Park. Best walked from Glympton to Church Enstone.

GLYMPTON

6 km (4 miles) N of Woodstock, off A44, on the River Glyme. Originally on the boundary of the Norman Forest, nowadays a well-wooded estate village. St Mary's Church, in Glympton Park, originally 13th century but thoroughly restored by G. E. Street in 1872, can be reached by footpaths (despite some ostentatious security). Almshouses, built as recently as 1949. After passing through hands of Australian buccaneer Alan Bond in 1990, the whole estate is being immaculately revived by present owner. PO stores. Glympton Park, with parkland, pasture and woodland, is surrounded by arable land and SW of A44 lies extensive woodland, much of it plantations now forming part of Kiddington Estate. Woodland, wetland and grassland in the parish provide valuable habitats for birds as well as a wide flora. Walks to the E of the river upstream to Kiddington or across the A44 into Glympton Wood.

HAILEY

3 km (2 miles) N of Witney, towards Charlbury. Literally, 'hay clearing'. Originally in three parts, Poffley End, Middletown and Delly End, the latter one of the prettiest places in West Oxfordshire. In the early middle ages, the 'Ends' must have led into the Forest woodland, subsequently cleared for agriculture. St John Evangelist Church, begun in 1866 to replace an earlier church of 1761, was described by G. E. Street, the then diocesan architect, as 'needlessly eccentric', but this is only true of its odd turret. Butcher and PO combined. The Lamb Inn with pub food, and The Bird In Hand PH with restaurant and accommodation at nearby Whiteoak Green. Hailey is situated in an undulating landscape, where Oxford clay meets oolitic limestone, with smallish fields enclosed by sometimes gappy hedges. Singe, or St John's, Wood is a large block of ancient woodland remaining to N of the parish with several small copses and green lanes elsewhere. Several public paths and quiet roads NE towards Ramsden, Wilcote and North Leigh, and NW by Singe Wood along ancient tracks towards Leafield.

IDBURY

8 km (5 miles) N of Burford, E of A424. From the Old English meaning 'Ida's fort', which was located on the brow of the hill towards the main road. St Nicholas Church has a Norman doorway and tympanum on its N side but mostly 14th century, with 15th-century windows on the S side. One or two substantial houses, including the Tudor manor house, once the home of the founder of *The Countryman* magazine, which was published in nearby Burford. Idbury commands wonderful views up and down the Evenlode valley. Small to medium sized fields, arable and grass – some of which retain their pattern of ridge and furrow – surround the village, with larger fields towards the A424. There are several small copses with Bould Wood, an ancient woodland, on the E parish boundary. Ancient woodland and limestone grassland and scrub are important habitats. Walks down into Bruern, or W into Nether Westcote and the New Inn, just in Gloucestershire.

KIDDINGTON

On river Glyme, 8 km (5 miles) NW of Woodstock. From Old English, 'son of Kidd's place'. A small estate village, originally on the boundary of the royal Forest. The Church of St Nicholas has Norman origins. Its apsidal E end was rebuilt by G. G. Scott in 1845. Kiddington Hall was remodelled by Charles Barry in 1850. Its parkland was designed by Capability Brown in about 1740, with formal garden features added in 1850s. The village, parkland, woodland and lake are surrounded beyond by large fields, with low sometimes gappy hedgerows. The parkland, with some ancient woodland, is an important habitat for flora, lichen and birds. Walks along the old road to Radford and then upstream to Clevely, or across the A44 towards Out Wood.

KINGHAM

On the Evenlode, 8 km (5 miles) W of Chipping Norton. From the Old English 'Caning's home'. Kingham was just outside the Norman Forest. St Andrew's Church was remodelled in 1852 and is more early Gothic Revival than earnest Victorian. The nearby Rectory, 1668, is a most handsome house. Pretty cottages and village green. Mill House Hotel and Restaurant, The Tollgate restaurant with accommodation, Plough Inn and Village Store and PO. Railway station 1 km S of the village with frequent trains to Oxford, London and Worcester. Nearby, the former Langston House Hotel is vigorous Jacobean revival in style. Woodland Trust community wood between the village and the station. Marsh habitat, S of the parish on the edge of the river, includes sneezewort, marsh marigold and meadowsweet.

LANGLEY

3 km (2 miles) SE of Shipton-under-Wychwood. Literally 'the long clearing'. In 13th and 14th centuries, the home of the Forester of Wychwood. Henry VII refurbished this as a royal hunting lodge serving the W of the Forest. His initial and that of his queen, Elizabeth of York, are carved in the surround of one of the Tudor windows. The area was cleared by 1857 and model Crown farms created. Nowadays TWR are based nearby. The remains of King John's Oak, a venerable forest tree, adjacent to the bridleway to NE.

LEAFIELD

4 km (3 miles) SE of Shipton-under-Wychwood. 'La Felde' in 1213. Literally a field or open clearing high in the ancient Forest woodlands. Known as Field Town until the 19th century. A long village, with a large green. Once a local source of pottery, hence 'Chimney end' where wood burning kilns were located. The powerful Church of St Michael was designed by Sir G. G. Scott in the late 1850s, and is a landmark throughout Wychwood. The parish was created at the time of the clearances, having been part of Shipton. The Spindlebury Inn and restaurant, The Fox PH with food and accommodation, PO and Village Stores. S of the village are small grassy fields with tall hedgerows. Elsewhere fields are larger and mostly arable. Small deciduous copses are scattered through the parish. An important local habitat is the limestone grassland in the dry valley SW of the village. Good walks N along Hatching Lane and past Kingstanding Farm, built after the 19th-century woodland clearances, and SE along Pay Lane to Whiteoak Green and beyond, or S from Lower End towards Crawley. On the Wychwood Way.

LONG HANBOROUGH

7 km (4 miles) NE of Witney on A4095 towards Woodstock. A long village with some modern development, it comprised the southern tip of the eastern sector of the medieval royal Forest. The George and Dragon PH and restaurant, Three Horse Shoes PH and The Bell PH with food are on the main road. The Swan PH on the Combe side of the village. Several shops. Frequent trains to Oxford, London and Worcester. Near the railway station is the Oxford Bus Museum. Access on foot into the S of Blenheim Park. Other walks around Pinsley Wood to Church Hanborough, and W through the village along Abel Wood to East End.

LYNEHAM

2 km (1.5 miles) N of Shipton-under-Wychwood. 'Lineham' in 1086, from the Old English meaning 'flax enclosure'. A humble village originally lying between Milton and Lyneham heaths. Golf course. Walks NE towards Merriscourt (a nearby hamlet with art gallery) and Sarsden.

MILTON-UNDER-WYCHWOOD

1km (0.5 miles) W of Shipton-under-Wychwood. From the Old English, meaning 'middle town'. Milton is a large living and working village with a green and cricket pitch at its centre. St Simon and St Jude Church, towards Bruern, by G. E. Street, 1854. Unusually for a Victorian church its simple exterior belies a spacious interior. Nearby former school and teacher's house also by Street, and later 'Queen Anne' vicarage by Jackson. Several shops, including butcher, Co-op, PO, builders merchants, and TV & hi-fi supplier. The Quart Pot PH with bar food and Hillborough House B&B. A hilly and undulating parish, rising from the clays by the River Evenlode to oolitic limestone at Milton Downs. Small grassy fields with neat hedgerows lie between the village and the river. Elsewhere, larger arable fields with some gappy hedges and walls. Several copses mark the horizon to SW. Important habitats are limestone grasslands above the village, and some calcareous fen fed by a series of streams in the SW of the parish. Walks NW towards Fifield, N along Oxfordshire Way to Bruern and E to Diggers community wood and Shipton.

MINSTER LOVELL

On river Windrush 5 km (3 miles) W of Witney. A priory was founded by Lovell's widow in 1206, but there must have been a pre-existing church of importance. The existing St Kenelm's Church was built in the 15th century and has a cruciform plan, central tower and spatially interesting interior. The nearby Hall, also 15th-century, was built by the 7th Lord Lovell and was formerly one of the great aristocratic houses of Oxfordshire until its 18th-century owner, the Earl of Leicestershire, sold off its stone and materials to pay for his new edifice at Holkham Hall, Norfolk. Now a romantic riverside ruin, managed by English Heritage. Interesting barn and dovecote nearby. Attractive thatched cottages line the village street, which leads to the Old Swan and restaurant. The Mill, with excellent modern vernacular additions, is now a conference centre. Nearby Charterville Allotments across the river were laid out idealistically in 1847 by Chartist leader Feargus O'Connor MP, with each cottage and smallholding having sufficient land for tenants from towns to maintain themselves – and to give the right to vote through possession of property. The scheme failed but the cottages remain. White Hart PH with food and accommodation, and New Inn PH. Spar grocery shop. The river cuts through the parish and its valley has small grassy fields divided by hedgerows, trees and woodland. Elsewhere are medium sized arable fields, with low sometimes gappy hedges. There are several woodland blocks in the Windrush valley and the valley lying immediately N of Little Minster. Important habitats include wet permanent pasture and marsh adjoining the river, valuable for wildfowl and marshland flora. Also limestone grasslands on the steeper slopes of the valley. Good walks down stream on S bank towards Witney, and on N bank towards Crawley.

NEW YATT

A small hamlet 1 km W of North Leigh. Saddlers Arms, with bar snacks. On the Wychwood Way.

NORTH LEIGH

4 km (3 miles) NE of Witney, N of A4095. The lower and older part of the village around the interesting Church of St Mary. Late Saxon tower, Norman nave, Early English work, Perpendicular Wilcote chapel (dedicated to the Wilcote family, an early 15th-century member of which was custodian of Cornbury Park), 15th-century wall painting of Last Judgement and a second N aisle by Christopher Kempster of Burford, one of Wren's masons at St Paul's. St Mary's is an architectural treasure chest. Remains of a windmill at the centre of the modern village. After enclosures in 1759, local rioters tore down hedges and fences and had to be subdued by the militia. The Woodman PH with food, and The Masons Arms PH with snacks. PO stores and Windmill Food Centre. An undulating parish, rising from Oxford clay in the S to oolitic limestone in the N. Mostly medium sized fields, both grass and arable, surrounded by hedgerows and trees. Cogges Wood and Eynsham Hall with its park, woodland and lake lie SE of A4095. North Leigh Common, near the main road towards Long Hanborough, belongs to West Oxfordshire District Council which is restoring this old heathland, a remnant of the large Eynsham Heath enclosed in 18th century. Important habitats also include biologically rich ancient woodland along valleys to N of parish, and several ponds and marshy areas. Interesting footpaths and lanes NW towards Wilcote and Holly Grove, and on W side of Eynsham Hall Park. On the Wychwood Way.

NORTHMOOR

Near the Thames, 3 km (2 miles) S of Stanton Harcourt. A flat parish almost surrounded by Thames and lower Windrush, the SE boundary of the Norman Forest. St Denis an unaltered and surprisingly spacious cruciform 14th-century church. Red Lion PH with food. Surrounding landscape is mostly grassland crossed by tree-lined watercourses and ditches. This dispersed village, still quiet, must have been very isolated until the coming of the motor car. Thames Path nearby.

PUDLICOTE

On the Evenlode, 2 km (1 mile) NE of Ascott-under-Wychwood. From the Old English meaning 'cottage by the puddle'. Nowadays a hamlet N of handsome Pudlicote House. Blocks of deciduous woodland to the N. The Wychwood Way passes nearby.

RAMSDEN

6 km (4 miles) N of Witney, off B4022. From the Old English meaning 'wild garlic valley' (or possibly simply 'rams valley'). The long and narrow village of pretty stone cottages leads down to a junction where Roman Akeman Street crossed this valley. St James Church, 1872, with picturesque spire. Royal Oak PH with food and accommodation. A hilly parish at its highest by Ramsden Heath. To the N of the parish are small grassy fields surrounded by prominent hedgerows. To the S of the village are larger arable fields, with occasionally gappy hedgerows. Several blocks of deciduous woods throughout the parish, some ancient. Important habitats include scarce acid scrub at Ramsden Heath and limestone grassland to the E of the parish. Several footpaths N towards Finstock and E along Akeman St towards Holly Grove and Wilcote. On the Wychwood Way.

SARSDEN

5 km (3 miles) SW of Chipping Norton. Sars Brook was probably a boundary of Wychwood Forest at Domesday. Sarsden House, remodelled about 1825, has a park by Repton. Several *cottages ornées* around the village. An undulating parish, rising from clay adjoining the River Evenlode and Sars Brook to limestone uplands above the small village. Small grassy tree-lined fields lie close to the village and near the brook. Elsewhere are larger arable fields. Many blocks of woodland, some of them ancient, others plantations and shelter belts. Important habitats include ancient woodland to the N of the parish adjoining Churchill, and Sarsden Park with woodland, lakes and streams which

support much bird life. Walks NE up the valley towards Sarsgrove Wood and S on the d'Arcy Dalton way towards Lyneham.

SHIPTON-UNDER-WYCHWOOD

6 km (4.5 miles) NE of Burford, towards Chipping Norton. From Old English, meaning 'sheep town'. Shipton was a royal manor at Domesday. Church of St Mary the Virgin, quite large and mostly 1200-50, originally the mother church for a parish which included Leafield, Ramsden, Lyneham and Milton, has a short tower with octagonal spire. Much of the the nearby village green was created as recently as 1960s. Between the church and the river Evenlode is the Prebendal House and Tithe Barn, now a retirement home. Shipton Court is one of the largest Jacobean houses in the country. One or two unusual modern houses built in 1960s, and a magnificent village hall built in 1998. The Shaven Crown, 15th-century, a hotel and restaurant; Lamb Inn with bar meals, restaurant and accommodation; Red Horse Inn with bar meals and rooms. Two shops, Costcutter and St Michael's Stores and PO. Very few trains stop at the station, N of the village towards Chipping Norton. Near the station the mill of F. W. P. Matthews Ltd. still grinds Cotswold corn. The parish rises from the river Evenlode to Shipton Down to the S. Near the river fields are mostly grassland, with good hedgerows and hedgerow trees. Elsewhere fields are larger, mostly arable, with some gappy stone walls. Several blocks of planted woodland near the village, including Diggers Wood planted in 2000 by the Woodland Trust and the people of Ascott, Shipton and Milton. Important limestone grassland habitats exist on roadside verges, especially towards Ascott-under-Wychwood, and also on railway embankment N of the village. The river margins support birdlife, including swans, herons and kingfishers. The Oxfordshire Way runs on the W side of the river towards Bruern, and on the N side towards Ascott-under-Wychwood.

SHORTHAMPTON

3 km (2 miles) W of Charlbury, off B4437, beyond the edge of today's Forest woodland. All Saints Church, simple and spiritual. Originally Norman, with 14th- and 15th-century wall paintings and 18th-century box pews. Walks S along a quiet road through the Forest, W to Ascott-under-Wychwood and E to Charlbury.

SOUTH LEIGH

4 km (3 miles) E of Witney, and S of A40. A large parish stretching from the River Windrush towards Cogges Wood. The village is small, with stone cottages. Church End is a pretty cul-de-sac. St James' Church,

originally Norman, with the finest group of medieval wall paintings in the county. Heavily restored in 19th century. Masons Arms PH with restaurant and rooms. Very gently rolling fields are a mixture of grass and arable, with a fairly intact pattern of hedgerows. Tar Wood and Cogges Wood are ancient Wychwood woodlands and there are numerous other small deciduous copses and green lanes. The ancient woodlands, parts of which are wet and support a wide range of flora and birdlife, are important habitats. Walk SW to Rushy Common and the River Windrush.

SPELSBURY

3 km (2 miles) N of Charlbury towards Chipping Norton. *Spelesberie* in 1086. 'Speol's stronghold'. Spelsbury is a quiet village, especially the cul-de-sac which leads down to All Saints Church. With Norman origins, this was rebuilt 1740-74 and contains interesting monuments to the Lees, and their descendants, of Ditchley. Almshouses 1688. Spelsbury is situated on the N side of the Evenlode valley, between two brooks which flow to the river. Caldron Mill, where the brooks meet, originated at least 1000 years ago. In their valleys are small fields, a mixture of grass and arable, surrounded by tall prominent hedgerows and strips of woodland. Above the village are larger fields, some with gappy walls and hedgerows. An ancient saltway runs through the N of the parish. Dean Grove, a block of ancient woodland, lies SW of the village, and to E of the parish are the plantations of Ditchley. There are a number of important wildlife habitats, including limestone grasslands on the roadside verges and green lanes. Marshy ground in the SW of the parish is rich in rush and sedge species. Dean Grove and newer plantations provide ornithological interest. Dean Common, the Wychwood Project's first community wood, which contains a variety of habitats, lies to W of the parish on restored sand pits. Walks E towards Taston and SW to Coldron Mill, Dean Grove, Dean Common and the Oxfordshire Way. The Wychwood Way runs through the NE of the parish.

STANTON HARCOURT

8 km (5 miles) SE of Witney, on B4499. The village is small, with thatched cottages and stone barns around the church and manor house at its centre. St Michael, originally Norman but remodelled in 13th century, contains many monuments to the Harcourt family. The spectacular 14th-century great kitchen and 15th-century NE tower remain of the Manor House, which was mostly demolished in about 1750. The Manor and garden, 12 acres with ancient ponds, are open

during the summer months. Harcourt Arms PH and restaurant. The Fox PH house on the edge of the village towards Eynsham. PO Stores. Stanton Harcourt is a flat parish between the Windrush and the Thames. SW of the village, Greenways, part of Hanson plc., are gradually landscaping the former gravel pits and hope to resurrect the Bronze Age henge monument, known as the Devil's Quoits, which was removed to make way for an airfield in Second World War. Vicarage Pit and Dix Pit, both SW of the village, are noted for their ornithological interest, and there is a small area of wet grassland and marsh adjacent to the Thames. A lane E of the village leads to a footpath passing through meadows to the Thames.

STONESFIELD

5 km (3 miles) SE of Charlbury. From the Old English, 'stunt's field', meaning stunted, or possibly fool's, field. Cotswold stone tiles, known in Oxfordshire as Stonesfield slates, were quarried and mined here from 16th until the beginning of the 20th century. St James, at the centre of the village, was a small Early English church before being quaintly restored and enlarged in the 19th century. Small village lock-up by churchyard gate. White Horse and Black Head PHs. Village store, and small PO near church. Stonesfield is on the oolitic limestone above the Evenlode. Except in a dry valley to the SW of the village, fields are large and arable, with gappy hedgerows and walls. Parts of the valley are wooded and there are plantations to the N of the parish. Some ancient woodland, limestone grassland and scrub in the valley are important habitats, and the old slate quarries contain exceptional fossils. Walks S across the Evenlode valley, NW along the Oxfordshire Way to Charlbury and NE along a footpath following Roman Akeman Street to Blenheim Park. On the Wychwood Way.

SWINBROOK

3 km (2 miles) E of Burford, on the River Windrush. Swinbrook is a very pretty small village with 17th- and 18th-century houses and cottages. Its name in Old English means 'the brook of swine'. Perhaps pigs were grazed in the Forest, remains of which still lie N towards South Lawn, the site of a former Forest lodge. St Mary's Church, mostly Decorated and Perpendicular, with interesting monuments and wood carving. The Mitford sisters are buried here. On one side of the river at the entrance to the village lies the pretty cricket field; on the other, The Swan Inn with food. Swinbrook is a hilly parish, with valleys running down to the river. Above the village fields are mostly medium sized arable, but surrounding the village and nearer the river fields are smaller, mostly

grassy, with prominent hedgerows. Considerable woodland exists N of the parish and around Dean Bottom, near the old medieval village of Widford. Important habitats are the ancient woodland to the N of the parish, which contains oak with an understorey of coppiced hazel, and marshy meadowland adjoining the Windrush. Riverside walks upstream to Widford and downstream to Asthall and Minster Lovell.

TASTON

A small hamlet 2 km (1.5 miles) N of Charlbury. Possibly from the 'Thor's stone', an ancient monolith still visible on the roadside verge opposite the stone cross. The Wychwood Way passes nearby.

TAYNTON

2 km (1.5 miles) NW of Burford, on the Windrush. *Teigntone* in 1086. Taynton is a pretty village of attractive houses, cottages and gardens. Stone from Taynton's former quarries built much of Oxford, Blenheim Palace, Windsor Castle and St Paul's. The Church of St John the Evangelist, mostly late Decorated and Perpendicular, with interesting gargoyles, lies to the S of the village towards the river. Hazelford Brook flows through the parish, from high land to the N down to the Windrush. Considerable woodland and disused quarries lie to the N of parish, with important habitats of limestone grassland, springs and ancient woodlands, and wet meadowlands near the Windrush, all important for birds. A footpath leads NW from the village up towards Tangley Hall and woods.

WALCOT

1 km (0.5 mile) W of Charlbury. Now a few houses, Walcot was a separate community in the Middle Ages. Its name means 'British, or Celtic, cottage'.

WIDFORD

2 km (1.5 miles) E of Burford. From the Old English, meaning 'willow ford'. Formerly a medieval village on the SW edge of Wychwood, nowadays a shrunken hamlet. 13th-century St Oswald's Church, built on the site of a Roman villa, lies in fields N of the river which show signs of the old village layout. Best approached on foot from Swinbrook.

WILCOTE

5 km (3.5 miles) of Witney, S of the River Evenlode. Literally 'Wifel's cottage'. Originally the site of a small Roman development along

Akeman St. A roman villa was excavated near Shakenoak Farm, but no remains are visible on the site. Wilcote is nowadays a small village consisting of Wilcote Manor, Wilcote House, Wilcote Grange and a few other dwellings. St Peter's is a small Norman Church, restored in the 19th century. An avenue of old pollarded ash trees leads to the ancient Ladywell, the site of ancient fertility rites. Former fishponds at Wilcote Grange Farm lie to S. The pretty, small scale, countryside has ancient woods N at Lady Grove and S at Holly Grove.

WINDRUSH

This river runs from near Winchcombe in Gloucestershire to Standlake in Oxfordshire where it joins the Thames at Newbridge. In Oxfordshire it was the SW boundary of Norman Wychwood. The floodplain is often a combination of wet permanent pasture and marsh, providing a particularly good habitat for waders and wildfowl.

WITNEY

On the A40, 16 km (10 miles) W of Oxford. 'Wita's island'. The river Windrush, which passes through the town, was the SW boundary of Wychwood Forest at Domesday. Famous since the Middle Ages for its blankets, there is still a blanket mill in Witney. The Blanket Hall, High Street, was built in 1721 for weighing and measuring blankets. St Mary's Church, 13th century, is spacious with a spectacular tower and spire. Nearby Church Green is the prettiest part of Witney but Corn Street, Market Place, the High Street and Wood Green are all very handsome. Remnants of the Bishop of Winchester's medieval palace lie E of the church. Cogges, originally a separate community across the river, with 14th-century St Mary's Church, and nowadays Cogges Manor Farm Museum (open late March–October). S of Witney a water park is being created and a footpath leads from Langel Common 10 km (6 miles) down the Windrush to its junction with the Thames near the Rose Revived PH on the A415 beyond Standlake. These meadowlands and marshy sites, prone to winter flooding, are valuable bird habitats. For further information on Witney, contact the Visitor Information Centre, Town Hall, Market Square, tel. 01993 775802.

WOODSTOCK

A bustling country town on the A44, 12 km (8 miles) NW of Oxford. Saxon kings are reputed to have had hunting lodges in the area. Henry I enclosed the first park at Woodstock and Henry II expanded this into a full scale royal palace. Open wood pasture from this park is still partly preserved around High Lodge and Combe Gate. By the 16th century the palace was falling into decay and in 1705 the manor of Woodstock was conferred on John Churchill, 1st Duke of Marlborough, for services to his country in the wars against France. His architect Vanbrugh built the magnificent Blenheim Palace between 1705 and 1717 and Capability Brown redesigned the grounds c.1764-74. Woodstock has many shops, restaurants, pubs and hotels. The Oxfordshire County Museum and Visitor Information Centre are based in Fletcher's House, Park Street, tel. 01993 811038. The landscape of this undulating parish is dominated by the town and Blenheim Park, cut by the River Glyme. The marshy habitats of the Glyme valley have a wide flora and are noted for their bird interest. On the Wychwood Way.

WOOTTON

3 km (2 miles) of Woodstock. Literally, 'a farmstead near the wood'. As its name suggests, originally on the edge of Wychwood. The Church of St Mary has Early English, Decorated, Perpendicular and Tudor work. King's Head Inn with restaurant and bed and breakfast; Killingworth Castle Inn with food and bed and breakfast. Wootton Stores and PO. This is a hilly parish, cut by the River Glyme. Dornford Lane, a bridleway to the E, was an ancient supply route between farmland at Steeple Barton and the Saxon royal manor at Woodstock. There are still many copses, green lanes and large hedgerows in the parish, and field sizes, especially in the valley, are small. Important habitats include limestone grassland on the steep banks in the centre of the parish, which have a number of orchid species, and the large reedbeds within the valleys of the rivers Glyme and Dorn. Wootton Wood, to the W of the parish, includes ancient woodland and provides good bird habitat.

SOURCES AND FURTHER READING

Oxfordshire Place Names, H. Alexander, Oxford, 1912.

The Place Names of Oxfordshire, M. Gelling, Cambridge, 1953/4.

The Buildings of England, Oxfordshire, Jennifer Sherwood and Nikolaus Pevsner, Penguin Books, 1974.

The New Oxfordshire Village Book, Oxfordshire Federation of WI's, Countryside Books, Newbury, 1990.

Blenheim, Landscape for a Palace, ed. James Bond and Kate Tiller, Alan Sutton, 1987.

Ditchley Park, Sir John Graham, English Life Publications Ltd., available from the Ditchley Foundation.

Parish Conservation Register, Nature Conservation Strategy for Oxfordshire, Oxfordshire County Council.

ILLUSTRATION CREDITS (by page number)

Ken Betteridge 90, 94
Craig Blackwell 79
Marc Dando 18, 26, 38, 39, 40, 42, 46
Michael Freeman 47
Amanda Henriques 65
Amanda Hopwood 128
Charles Keighley 55, 58, 77, 96, 104, 112, 113, 115, 116, 117, 118, 121, 122, 125
North Leigh School 103
Beryl Schumer 27, 28, 30, 36
Alan Spicer 25, 60, 74, 75, 77, 78, 81 (top), 82, 83, 84, 91, 92, 93, 95, 97, 123, 126
Louise Spicer 13, 69, 76, 81, 124, 131, 136, 139
David West 119
Wychwood Project 20/21, 101, 105, 107

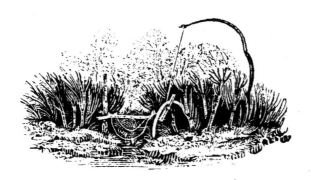